40 DAYS OF
HOPE

40 DAYS OF HOPE

LACEY BUCHANAN
with BETHANY JETT

CHARISMA
HOUSE

Most CHARISMA HOUSE BOOK GROUP products are available at special quantity discounts for bulk purchase for sales promotions, premiums, fund-raising, and educational needs. For details, write Charisma House Book Group, 600 Rinehart Road, Lake Mary, Florida 32746, or telephone (407) 333-0600.

40 DAYS OF HOPE by Lacey Buchanan with Bethany Jett
Published by Charisma House
Charisma Media/Charisma House Book Group
600 Rinehart Road
Lake Mary, Florida 32746
www.charismahouse.com

This book or parts thereof may not be reproduced in any form, stored in a retrieval system, or transmitted in any form by any means—electronic, mechanical, photocopy, recording, or otherwise—without prior written permission of the publisher, except as provided by United States of America copyright law.

Unless otherwise noted, Scripture quotations are taken from the Holy Bible, New International Version®, NIV®. Copyright © 1973, 1978, 1984, 2011 by Biblica, Inc.™ Used by permission of Zondervan. All rights reserved worldwide. www.zondervan.com. The "NIV" and "New International Version" are trademarks registered in the United States Patent and Trademark Office by Biblica, Inc.™

Scripture quotations marked ESV are from the Holy Bible, English Standard Version. Copyright © 2001 by Crossway Bibles, a division of Good News Publishers. Used by permission.

Scripture quotations marked GNT are from the Good News Translation. Copyright © 1992 by American Bible Society.

Scripture quotations marked MEV are from the Modern English Version. Copyright © 2014 by Military Bible Association. Used by permission. All rights reserved.

Scripture quotations marked NASB are from the New American Standard Bible, copyright © 1960, 1962, 1963, 1968, 1971, 1972, 1973, 1975, 1977, 1995 by The Lockman Foundation. Used by permission. (www.Lockman.org)

Scripture quotations marked NCV are taken from the New Century Version®. Copyright © 2005 by Thomas Nelson. Used by permission. All rights reserved.

Scripture quotations marked NKJV are taken from the New King James Version®. Copyright © 1982 by Thomas Nelson. Used by permission. All rights reserved.

Scripture quotations marked NLT are from the Holy Bible, New Living Translation, copyright © 1996, 2004, 2007. Used by permission of Tyndale House Publishers, Inc., Wheaton, IL 60189. All rights reserved.

Copyright © 2017 by Lacey Buchanan
All rights reserved

Cover design by Justin Evans

Visit the author's website at http://christianbuchanan.blogspot.com.

Library of Congress Cataloging-in-Publication Data:
An application to register this book for cataloging has
been submitted to the Library of Congress.
International Standard Book Number:
978-1-62999-477-2
E-book ISBN: 978-1-62999-149-8

The author has attempted to recreate events, locales,
and conversations from her memories of them. Some
names and identifying details have been changed to
protect the privacy of those individuals.

Portions of this book were previously published by
Charisma House as *Through the Eyes of Hope*, ISBN
978-1-62999-107-8, copyright © 2017.

While the author has made every effort to provide
accurate Internet addresses at the time of publication,
neither the publisher nor the author assumes any
responsibility for errors or for changes that occur
after publication.

17 18 19 20 21 — 987654321
Printed in the United States of America

CONTENTS

	Introduction xi
Day 1	Rise on Eagles' Wings 1
Day 2	Spiritual Blindness 6
Day 3	Blessed Be the Name of the Lord 10
Day 4	God Is Still Good 15
Day 5	God Knows What He's Doing 20
Day 6	We Walk by Faith, Not Sight 26
Day 7	Think on Higher Things 31
Day 8	God Is Unchanging 36
Day 9	Look Beyond Your Circumstances 40
Day 10	Questioning God 44
Day 11	Put Your Trust in God 48
Day 12	Mysterious Ways 53
Day 13	You Are Awesome 58
Day 14	Sacrifice Takes Many Forms 62

40 Days of Hope

Day 15	Holding Fast to God's Promises	67
Day 16	Ribbons of Prayer	71
Day 17	Letting Go and Letting God	76
Day 18	Holy Boldness	80
Day 19	Train-Wreck Moments	85
Day 20	When God Allows the Pain	89
Day 21	Quiet Faith	93
Day 22	Weeping Into Joy	98
Day 23	Our Ever-Present Help	102
Day 24	The Blessing of Friendship	106
Day 25	The Small Things	111
Day 26	Dealing With Setbacks	115
Day 27	The Gift of No	120
Day 28	Sticks and Stones	125
Day 29	God the Restorer	129
Day 30	You Are His Masterpiece	133
Day 31	The Power of Community	137
Day 32	Willing to Learn	142
Day 33	God Looks at the Heart	146

Day 34	At Work Behind the Scenes	150
Day 35	Modern-Day Miracles	154
Day 36	Step Out	159
Day 37	World-Changers	163
Day 38	The Myth of Control	167
Day 39	Choosing Forgiveness	172
Day 40	Redemption	177
	Conclusion	183
	Notes	185

INTRODUCTION

"What is life but God's daring invitation to a remarkable journey?"[1]

It's full of ups and downs, twists and turns, joyful memories, and bitter tragedies. My husband, Chris, and I prayed that our firstborn, Christian, would be healed of the birth defect the doctors saw when he was still *in utero*, but God allowed him to be born with a cleft palate so severe his eyes didn't even form. Yet through our journey of loving and raising our amazing son, we have learned more about our heavenly Father's love and provision than either of us could ever have dreamed.

In this book I share many of those truths, truths that have helped us love more, worry less, and see God in the midst of our adversities. Our hope is that this forty-day prayer journey strengthens your faith, renews your belief in God's power, and simultaneously heals your heart of any wounds.

In Scripture the number forty is often connected to new beginnings, freedom from captivity, and victory over adversaries. Frequently, when God wanted to bring transformation, the process lasted forty days.

My prayer is that the next forty days will bring a change for you as well.

Let this book do much more than decorate your nightstand. Use the space provided or a notebook to respond to the questions. Scribble in the margins. Highlight and underline passages that touch your heart.

Joy does come in the morning.

His mercies are renewed each day.

You are worthy of God's favor.

I invite you to take this journey with me for the next forty days…and delight in how God transforms your heart.

Day 1

RISE ON EAGLES' WINGS

But those who wait upon the LORD shall renew their strength; they shall mount up with wings as eagles, they shall run and not be weary, and they shall walk and not faint.
—ISAIAH 40:31, MEV

LIFE CAN BE scary.

I felt like my world unraveled when my husband, Chris, and I learned the severity of our firstborn son Christian's birth defect and disability. Our marriage turned rocky, I struggled with the work-mom balance, money was beyond tight, and I felt completely alone.

There were times when I felt exhausted both physically and spiritually. I wanted to believe without wavering that God was who He said He was and would walk with me through this nightmare. But I couldn't be strong on my own. I needed to remind myself that God had always been faithful and He wouldn't stop now.

I needed a tangible reminder, so I developed a habit of writing Bible verses onto index cards. I placed them all around my house to help remind me of God's power and provision for my family and me. Sometimes I'd forget that I'd put a card in a drawer, so time after time I'd find one randomly. It was always the most perfect timing.

I'm convinced that from the moment I wrote them down, God knew exactly which words I was going to need, and when and where I would later find the card.

One instance sticks out to me. After a particularly rough day I pulled into a parking space and drew a deep breath to somehow gather the strength I needed. I reached into my purse, and my fingers brushed against one of the index cards. I read the verse and immediately felt God's presence. Just when I needed it, God gave me a verse that helped me refocus and find the strength to get through that day.

The Bible says in Isaiah 40:31 that those who wait upon the Lord will renew their strength; they will mount up with wings like eagles.

Waiting on the Lord isn't a passive kind of waiting. We aren't sitting in a metaphorical waiting room, reading old magazines to pass the time. The waiting mentioned in Isaiah refers to an active waiting with hope and expectation that God is going to meet our needs. As children of God, we should have enough confidence in our Father's character and goodness to believe that He will provide for us.

When we wait upon Him, our strength will be renewed. Isaiah uses a word picture to better communicate this idea. He says we will mount up on wings like eagles.

This is incredible imagery, one that God uses several times in Scripture. Besides the reference in Isaiah 40, God tells Moses in Exodus 19:3–4 to remind the people that He delivered them from Egypt "on eagles' wings."

I've seen eagles soar on television shows, but I can only imagine how beautiful it would be to see an eagle take flight in person. They are magnificent creatures worthy of being the national symbol for the United States.

Eagles are frequently symbols of power, strength, and transcendence because they can fly higher than any other species of bird. Not only do they have a wide wingspan, but also they don't spend their time flapping furiously as many birds do. Eagles will soar until they reach great heights, and then they'll just glide. This allows them to cover long distances without expending much energy, resting their wings in the process.[1]

While many birds will look for shelter when a

storm is passing through, eagles take advantage of the winds to lift them higher, often flying above the storm. In doing so, they find rest.[2]

Often we go through life fluttering our wings trying to complete our to-do lists or be everything our families need us to be or merely keep our heads above water.

We flap instead of glide. And the effort is exhausting.

Chris and I have learned that if we choose to trust in the Lord, He will renew our strength. And He will help us soar—above our weariness, above the storm clouds circling around us, even above our fears of the unknown.

It's no secret that life brings difficulty. Even Jesus said in John 16:33 that we will have troubles. However, He also said He has overcome the world. When we're weary, our God will renew our strength, and He will see us through every storm.

SEE GOD...

Sometimes we have to remind ourselves of God's promises and provision. Keeping a journal or diary of prayer requests and praises is an excellent discipline. When hard times come, you can flip through and remember how God delivered you in the past, and you can build your faith that He will definitely help you again.

What difficult circumstances has God walked through with you?

_____

_____

_____

_____

_____

_____

_____

GIVE IT TO GOD IN PRAYER

Dear God, You are my hope, and I choose to put my trust in You. Please let me feel Your presence today. When I don't know what steps to take, I ask for You to guide me. I trust that You want the best for Your children, and I know You will only lead me in straight paths. In Jesus's name, amen.

Day 2

SPIRITUAL BLINDNESS

I will lead the blind by ways they have not known, along unfamiliar paths I will guide them; I will turn the darkness into light before them and make the rough places smooth. These are the things I will do; I will not forsake them.
—Isaiah 42:16

Christian was born blind, but there was a metaphorical darkness that seemed to hover over Chris and me. We felt confused as we waited constantly in hospital rooms without knowing exactly what we were waiting for. I felt "blind" in the sense that I didn't know where I was heading. I didn't know what I was doing or how I was going to get to the next place.

I couldn't see any further than my next step, and sometimes that was even hard to decipher. I felt like everything I thought I knew about God was wrong and that He wasn't anywhere near this dark and heavy place.

Spiritual Blindness

It was terrifying, to be honest. I was so scared, but what made it worse was that everyone around me was scared as well. No one had answers, really. Doctors tried to offer some solutions, but Christian's medical condition confused them, and I knew that for many things, they were making educated guesses at best.

Chris was as consumed by the dark grief as I was, and he didn't have any more answers than I did. My parents were there supporting us, and like a child I looked to them, hopeful they could give me solutions, but they couldn't provide what I longed for. They were grieving too.

It was an isolating and lonely experience. But the thing is, I was never really alone.

If God is anywhere, He is in the midst of our grief. He cares when His children hurt. My heavenly Father is a good and faithful parent. He didn't fix the problems I was facing, but He stood with me through them.

Looking back, I wish I had been more conscious of His presence during those times. But because I have been through the hard times without paying close attention to how God was working, I am all the more aware of His presence in the hard times we face now. Whenever Christian has a surgery, I can feel God's presence, as if He's sitting in that hospital waiting room with us. Because He is.

The promise of God in Isaiah 42 is clear. He says,

"This is what I will do: lead, guide, transform, and make smooth." When we were unbelievers, Christ died for us (Rom. 5:8). We are blind spiritually when we don't know God, when we don't know the awe-inspiring truth of Jesus's sacrifice on the cross.

This verse in Isaiah is one of my absolute favorites.

Following Jesus means we have spiritual sight. It means we know we will not be forsaken. It means our eternity is secure through Christ our Lord.

Our God is the one who opens the eyes of the blind. He will turn our darkness into light and smooth the road ahead.

SEE GOD...

Do you live like your eyes are spiritually opened, or do circumstances blind you? In what area(s) of your life do you need God to turn darkness into light?

___

___

___

___

___

Spiritual Blindness

GIVE IT TO GOD IN PRAYER

Father, though life can be dark and my path unclear, let me remember that You are always with me. When darkness looms, help me to declare Your promise that You will never leave me or forsake me. Keep my path straight and my feet planted on the firm foundation of Jesus Christ, no matter how hard the storms might press against me. Father, You are my hope and my peace in the midst of the darkest night. In Jesus's name, amen.

Day 3

BLESSED BE THE NAME OF THE LORD

He said, "Naked I came from my mother's womb, and naked will I return there. The Lord gave, and the Lord has taken away; blessed be the name of the Lord."
—Job 1:21, MEV

Is there really any way to measure loss?

In the Old Testament Job experienced tragedy after tragedy, and yet his righteous heart stayed pure toward God. I can't imagine the emotional pain Job went through. To lose even one child is unimaginable, let alone an entire family and one's livelihood. And yet I complain over the small #firstworldproblems that affect most of us. Traffic is heavy. The drive-through line is too long. My phone battery died.

When God blessed Chris and me with our firstborn, we expected a perfect child, our strange new-parent fear being that he wouldn't have the requisite number of toes. Yet early in our pregnancy we learned that while Christian had all ten piggies intact, there were serious issues happening *in utero*. Because of an extremely rare birth defect, he was born with a severe Tessier cleft lip and palate, which caused parts of his face to be missing. His eyes didn't even form.

Heaven knows we prayed for God to heal our baby, but for whatever reason that I can't possibly understand this side of heaven, God chose to let the disability stand.

God blessed us with an amazing son, but He allowed, *not caused*, Christian to have a birth disorder.

I've often thought that perhaps there is another side to this. Perhaps God did answer our prayer to heal Christian. Perhaps Christian's condition was life-threatening, but because our God is gracious, He spared Christian's life.

Perhaps the cleft, which is already severe enough to be classified as one-in-fifty documented cases in the world, would have been worse. Maybe God heard our prayers and intervened to the point that what we see as a negative was actually God saying, "Yes, I hear you. I love you. I will help you."

Oftentimes people will say, "God won't give you more than you can handle," but I disagree. In Job's story God gave Satan almost full rein; Satan's only clause: you must spare Job's life. What was heaped upon Job was way more than one person can handle. And honestly, there are things worse than death.

I'm not questioning the call God made regarding Job, but I think we're wrong to say that God won't give us more than we can bear. I don't see that in Scripture. What I see is Jesus saying, "Give Me your burdens and I will give you rest for your soul." (See Matthew 11:29–30.)

There's a lot we can't handle on our own. But that's kind of the point. God doesn't want us to try to handle the good, the bad, or the ugly life throws at us without Him.

Sometimes it can feel like we're, according to Ann-with-an-e Shirley from Green Gables, in the "depths of despair," walking our road of suffering all alone. But we're not alone. The God we serve is not only there walking with us, but He also knows exactly how we feel.

We don't often think of Jesus as a sorrowful man, but the Bible says we serve a God who understands our pain. Isaiah 53:3 says that Jesus was "despised and rejected by men, a man of sorrows and acquainted with grief" (MEV).

Jesus understands what we go through. He knows how it feels to experience pain. He was mocked, beaten, and crucified, yet He trusted our heavenly Father in the midst of the suffering.

In the stories of Job and Jesus we see two examples of great suffering, yet their response was to praise and trust God.

In our darkest circumstances there is always hope. When there is heartache and troubled times ahead, we must choose to bless the name of the Lord.

SEE GOD...

According to Scripture "Blessed be the name of the Lord" is the appropriate response for when God "gives and takes away." What is your first inclination when hard times come, and how can you change your response to bless His name through the tears?

_____

_____

_____

_____

_____

_____

_____

Give It to God in Prayer

Dear God, I want to bless Your name both when You give and when You take away. Help me to remember to praise You through the good and the bad, and that You are worthy in both. In Jesus's name, amen.

Day 4

GOD IS STILL GOOD

Even if He doesn't save us, He is still good.
—Daniel 3:18, author's paraphrase

Log into Facebook at any given time, and you'll see statuses such as, "Got the test results back today and everything is fine. God is good." Yes, we absolutely should praise God for healing and for great health. I'm all about that. But part of me thinks that even if those test results didn't come back OK, God is still good and worthy to be praised.

Even if we hear the worst news in the world, God is *still* good.

But that wasn't always my response.

We'd been prepared for how bad Christian's birth defect would be. The doctors warned us, but I prayed hard for a miracle. In fact, when I was pregnant, I dreamed that I was on a stage in front of a huge crowd—a sea of people as far as I could see. I was holding Christian with his back to me, like Simba in the movie *The Lion King*, showing him off to the multitude below.

I wasn't giving an eloquent speech. Instead, I was shouting my praise to the onlookers. My voice was strong, and I couldn't stop smiling. "Look what God did for my baby. This was *God*!" I'd seen a miracle happen, and I was showing the proof to the world. When I woke up, my heart was still beating wildly. I laid my hands on my pregnant belly, the closest I could get to my unborn child, and I knew—just *knew*—that the dream was God's way of letting me know He would heal Christian.

I had peace. So many Bible verses were comforting to me, and I knew that God had this covered. I believe God had the power to heal Christian before he was born. But in our case He chose not to.

Honestly, when Christian was born with an extremely rare birth defect, I wasn't praising God. My mind couldn't comprehend how such a rare birth disorder that clefted my baby's eyes could be good. It seemed as if the Bible's promises that I'd clung to during my pregnancy weren't true.

How is Christian's birth defect *good*?

I felt betrayed.

I'd put my faith and trust in God wholeheartedly. I *knew* Christian would be healed. Yet he wasn't.

Now, looking back, I can see what that dream meant.

As I mentioned in *Through the Eyes of Hope*, God made it clear to me that I would not hide this baby. God has graciously given us this platform to declare the goodness of God's works, the beauty of His creation, through Christian.

Literally I had to blindly trust God when nothing in our circumstances looked good. I viewed the situation from a lens of pain and betrayal, so it was a slow lesson to trust God after I felt like He'd ignored my pleas of, "God, please heal my baby." But God slowly changed my perception from "God lied to me; He isn't good," to "God's promises are truth even if they don't look like we think they should."

If God had shown me the whole picture (most of which we haven't experienced yet) and asked my permission to allow Christian to have a birth defect, even knowing what I know now, I would have said no. I never would have agreed to this, and yet my faith has been strengthened in a way that it never would have been if Chris and I hadn't walked this road.

I wish I could say that I'm thankful for this difficult journey. I want to say, "Yes, God, I'll walk the road gladly if it means we'll bring You glory." And I'd like to think if it was just my life being affected, I may choose that. However, when your child is involved, it's like a switch is flipped. All bets are off. Nothing else matters but his protection and safety. It's another reminder that

Jesus's death on the cross was beyond heart wrenching for God the Father.

I wish I'd had the faith of Shadrach, Meshach, and Abednego from the beginning. When they faced imminent death, they said, "Our God can save us, but even if He doesn't, He is still good."

That's not an easy thing, to believe that God is good when we're in pain or crisis. But isn't the essence of faith to believe God is who He says He is no matter what the situation looks like? Whether we're praying through smiles or tears, we can trust that God is always faithful, always loving, always working things together for our good (Rom. 8:28), because that's His character. God isn't human like us. He doesn't choose to be good or loving or faithful. He *is* love, goodness, and faithfulness. It's His perfect nature.

So whether or not our circumstances feel good, God is still good...because good is who He is.

SEE GOD...

We need to choose to praise God in the midst of our circumstances, whether it be during health trials, financial hardships, or familial relationships that get strained. It's not our typical human response, so how can we look at hard times and bring God glory though them?

GIVE IT TO GOD IN PRAYER

Father, let Your praise always be on my lips. When things look bad, remind me that You are not defined by my circumstances. Father, when my hopes and dreams fall flat, when You answer me with a "no" or a "not yet," when things don't go the way I think they should, You are still good. You are worthy of my praise. Amen.

Day 5

GOD KNOWS WHAT HE'S DOING

The heart of man plans his way, but the LORD establishes his steps.
—PROVERBS 16:9, ESV

I'VE KNOWN I was going to be a lawyer since I was eight years old. If you'd asked me at age seven, "Lacey, what do you want to be when you grow up?," my response would have been, "Ballerina. Veterinarian. Teenage Mutant Ninja Turtle."

You may call me Michelangelo.

When I was in second grade, we had a guest come to our classroom to talk about colleges and universities. I'm proud to be the first person in my family to graduate from college, but at that time I'd never heard the word before, and I thought the whole idea sounded *fantastic*.

I came home and promptly announced, "I want to go to college."

My mom looked at me. "That's great, but I don't know how we would pay for it."

Ever the optimist I said, "That's OK. I don't need you to pay for it. I'll pay for it myself."

Today there are a lot of scholarships, but back then the only kids who went to college had parents who could afford it. I had no idea how much it would cost, but I knew I wanted it, and I was determined to make it happen.

I worked really hard during high school, scored high on the ACT test, and got a full ride to Middle Tennessee State University. A session with a career coach confirmed that everything pointed me toward law. So I declared my major as pre-law and hit the books. All my friends were involved with intramural sports, so I played one season, but then became the girl who got teased for staying home all the time to study.

In terms of law school I knew I didn't want to practice criminal defense or personal injury law. If someone asked what I wanted to do with my degree specifically though, I didn't really know. I thought maybe family law, but I wasn't certain. It didn't encompass enough and wasn't deep enough.

I had my plans laid out. But God directed the path.

After Christian was born, I was still working and attending law school full time. With all of the therapies and doctor's appointments Christian needed, I was ready to quit my dream and drop out of law school. I couldn't handle all the stress.

That's where God stepped in.

God established my steps one day while I was sitting in my mental health law class, stressed to the max. I wasn't paying attention to the lesson, honestly. I was thinking about all the things on the next day's agenda, and I felt daunted and overwhelmed.

The professor was discussing the ins and outs of mental health. Typically, in my other classes, I felt like legal jargon was a different language—what in the world is a *tort*? But on this day all those keywords were familiar: SSI, *guardian ad litem*, conservatorships.

I understood what the professor was saying because I already knew this world, from the side of a parent. The side of a potential client.

I realized I wasn't the only one who had these needs. These were the topics I could address if I had this degree. There were people out there who could use my help, people *just like me*.

It was in that moment in my mental health law class that I knew I was meant to go into disability law. In that *aha* moment I felt like the last fifteen years of my life all came together, and I could see how God had lined up everything and prepared me for this. This was in His plans all along; I just wasn't privy to it until that moment.

God Knows What He's Doing

When God and I work together, we're a fearsome team. *wink.*

It would have been amazing if I could have already gone through law school and passed the bar before experiencing the roadblocks, paperwork overload, and miles of legal and medical red tape we faced after Christian was born. The journey may have been smoother if I'd already been given the knowledge I would need to handle the legal side of my baby's disability.

For whatever reason, God saw fit to let two crucial life experiences intersect, winding and weaving around each other like threads woven into fabric. If you have ever cross-stitched, you learn that the skill of the stitcher doesn't come from how beautiful the front looks, but what the threads look like when you turn it over.

The cross-stitch of Christian's pregnancy and early years may look smooth and well-done on the surface, but if you flip the tapestry, you'll see clusters where the threads of my temperament and patience broke and had to be re-knotted and different colored strands where Chris and I intersected and then railroaded into parallel paths.

It's messy. And ugly. And broken.

But the beautiful thing is that God heals, and when we look at the front, a beautiful picture emerges as we follow His directions. No one may ever turn over our fabric to see the construction that happened behind the scenes, but God can use even a tangled mess of broken thread to create a lovely tapestry.

When we follow the will of the Designer, we see that God has a masterpiece planned. He's waiting for us to follow His direction, one stitch (or step) at a time.

See God

Looking back over your life, what are specific ways you see God weaving together your purpose? Do you see ways He has prepared you for hard times ahead?

_____

_____

_____

_____

_____

_____

_____

GIVE IT TO GOD IN PRAYER

Father, give me wisdom and discernment to listen for Your guidance and direction. Keep me on the path You have laid out for me, and if I should stray, redirect me. I have made my own plans in life, but Lord, You direct my steps. Direct me to where You want me. In Jesus's name, amen.

Day 6

WE WALK BY FAITH, NOT SIGHT

Now faith is confidence in what we hope for and assurance about what we do not see.... By faith we understand that the universe was formed at God's command.
—Hebrews 11:1, 3

Have you ever stumbled through a pitch-black room, searching with your fingers along the wall for a light switch or frantically waved your arms in front of you as you reach for a fan's light cord? Even if I'm in a familiar place, if it's dark, I step cautiously so I don't fall over an ottoman or stub my toes against furniture. Let's face it; I can trip over things even if I do see them.

Living in physical darkness is Christian's way of life. He doesn't know any different, just that he lives in a world that he doesn't fully understand, a world not exactly made for him.

Now that he's getting older, he will map out a new room, taking small steps as he learns the layout. This year he began using a white cane to direct in front of his feet, like a conductor leading an orchestra, although he prefers to use it as a light saber or sword and fight his little brother.

Even though he can't see what's coming, Christian bravely forges ahead. Without his eyesight he can't anticipate what's coming in an unfamiliar atmosphere. However, that doesn't hinder his love for exploring a new place and the innocent curiosity with which he learns about the world around him.

Seeing the world from Christian's perspective, my family and I have learned firsthand that sight is a convenience, but not a necessity. Even without his vision Christian still gets where he wants to go. He may not do it as quickly or as easily as everyone else, but no one said we all had to move at the same pace.

Spiritually I walked in darkness while Chris and I navigated this new world of how to care for an infant with a severe cleft and no eyesight. I didn't know where to go, so I took baby steps, reaching out for anyone who would guide me. Because I initially trusted in other people instead of God, I ended up with a lot of emotional bruising as I whacked into insurance issues, misdiagnoses, and overwhelming fatigue and stress.

It wasn't until I let God lead me that things started to turn around. I don't mean that Christian was suddenly healed, but even though I couldn't see where God was leading, I stopped being so apprehensive. If God said, "Step here," I would. If He said, "Jump there," I did.

The biggest lesson I've learned is that I don't have to see in order to trust Him; I only need to walk. The Bible says that we walk by faith, not by sight, but this never made as much sense to me as it does now. So often I could not see where God was leading me or where I was headed, and it was terrifying. But just as I lead Christian through this world because he needs me to guide him, so will my Father lead me where I need to go.

God says in Isaiah 42:16 that He will lead the blind by ways they have not known, and that He will make the rough places smooth. While God doesn't tell me everything I want to know or snap His fingers to fix all my problems, He does guide me safely to His intended destination for my life.

I was so scared during Christian's early days of life, terrified of taking the wrong step or even where the "right" step would lead to next. Yet God always led me through and stayed by me as I walked.

I don't need to have all the answers. I don't have to

know what God is doing. Just as Christian takes my hand and trusts me to get him safely to his destination, we only have to trust in our heavenly Father to do the same.

SEE GOD...

Are there times in your life when you've had to completely walk by faith? What are some specific ways that you *know* God is leading you? What are the terrifying parts of walking through life without being able to see too far ahead?

_____

_____

_____

_____

_____

_____

_____

Give It to God in Prayer

Father, You are the one who opens blind eyes. When I can't see, help me to trust in You and allow You to lead me. When I stumble onto my own paths, lead me back to You. In Jesus's name, amen.

Day 7

THINK ON HIGHER THINGS

Finally, brothers and sisters, whatever is true, whatever is noble, whatever is right, whatever is pure, whatever is lovely, whatever is admirable—if anything is excellent or praiseworthy—think about such things.
—Philippians 4:8

Parents love new baby milestones, such as when their kid rolls over, sits up on his own, and takes his first step. We assumed Christian would walk, but at eighteen…nineteen…twenty-one months old he still wasn't walking.

When he finally took his first steps at twenty-seven months, we celebrated as if we'd won the lottery. With all that Christian has been through, everything feels like a big deal and all the more reason to rejoice.

Those who follow us on Facebook see us celebrating

Christian's milestones or fun wins in our journey—like Christian playing Bop-It!, *which is thrilling for me*—but some people also see a little boy with tissue where his eyes should be. And this saddens them. Despite all the wonderful things I share, I receive comments all the time from people asking, "How can you be so happy?"

They think my son should bring me sorrow. But it's just the opposite. He brings me joy.

Recently we dined at a restaurant in Pigeon Forge, Tennessee. Christian sat on my lap, cracking up over something he thought was funny. In fact, he was laughing so hard that a woman stopped us on the way out and commented, "You sure do have a happy boy there."

We do. Laughter is our normal, though those who are new to our story have a hard time believing we have anything to rejoice over.

When strangers see Christian for the first time, empathy tugs at their heart strings, and they assume I feel the same way they do. It's hard for people to understand that I've already lived through the initial emotional roller coaster of fear, followed by sadness, followed by more fear.

The only way I survive is to focus on all of our blessings.

It's like in the story of Pollyanna. She was a little orphaned girl with everything in life going against her.

Sent to live with her stodgy aunt, Pollyanna delights the entire community with her willingness to always see the good in every one. She looked for the silver lining even during her darkest days.

Pollyanna has the same philosophy I do. I look for the silver lining.

The worst-case scenarios for Chris and me have already been played out. Our hearts were already broken when we learned the severity of Christian's cleft. We've already mourned our losses.

So now we find joy in Christian's giggles. We find peace when he sleeps soundly, not a care in the world, snuggled into the crook of his daddy's arms. We feel God's mercy when we hear Christian say, "Mama," or play the piano.

We find joy in the small moments because those are what build up into the best memories. The hard times came, and more are on the horizon; we don't deny that. But because of God's love we can get through them. If we train our minds to accept the difficult news, we can process it and, somehow in our hearts, place it in God's strong and capable hands.

We focus on what good is there, even when it's hard to find.

We feel blessed that Christian's condition, as severe as it is, isn't worse. We thank God that he is learning to talk, and we praise Him for the intelligence we're daily observing in our little boy. We're grateful that our second son was spared a disability, and we are thankful that God continues to bless our family.

Sometimes when hard times come our way, the blow can leave us shaken. Our world becomes small and dark, and it feels unnatural to think there are people walking around untainted by the evil that rocked our "normal." On some days we can't think of the lovely things because, in our minds, they don't exist.

On those days when the road looks rough, it can be difficult to follow the guidance of Philippians 4:8. It can be hard to find the lovely among the ashes. When our worst fears come to life, it can feel impossible to focus on things worthy of praise. But during those hard times we have to remind ourselves that God loves us, and we must force our minds to think on better things because that's how the Holy Spirit will be able to pull us out of the darkness.

Yes, there are things in this world with the power to hurt us. But as we keep our minds focused on what God wants us to focus on—things that are worthy of praise—the truth will begin to sink into our hearts and change our perspective.

SEE GOD...

Some seasons of life are harder than others. Looking back on recent or the most difficult trials in your life, what are the areas where you can see how God watched out for you?

___

___

___

___

GIVE IT TO GOD IN PRAYER

Father, life can be hard. Some days are overwhelming and draining. But You have promised that You will always be with us, and that You give us a peace that passes all understanding. When the hard days come, Father, remind me of those promises. When the days are easy, Father, remind me to give You praise. In all things, Father, help me to focus on what is true, honorable, just, pure, lovely, commendable, excellent, and worthy of praise. Father, help me keep my eyes on You. Hard days will come, but they will also pass. Keep my eyes fixed on You. In Jesus's name, amen.

Day 8

GOD IS UNCHANGING

I the Lord do not change; therefore you, O children of Jacob, are not consumed.
—Malachi 3:6, esv

After I received the call that we had to go back for a follow-up ultrasound, Chris and I drove separately so he could get back to work. It was only a fifteen-minute drive, but the songs that came on the radio were full of hope and promise. Everything was going to be OK.

I walked into that doctor's office confident.

I left shattered.

My baby had a problem, and *God knew* this was coming. He knew.

It wasn't surprising to Him that we were going to hear devastating news about our baby. That day changed our entire lives, and the God who created the universe from His spoken word, the God who shaped man out of dust, the God who listens to my prayers and holds my heartache in His hands is the same God who drew me close that day, even as I struggled to trust Him.

"For I am the LORD, I do not change; therefore you, O sons of Jacob, are not consumed" (Mal. 3:6, MEV). When I read that verse months after that fateful day, those words shook my heart. My faith was weak, but God wasn't the One who changed. He was the same. I was the one moving away from Him when life took a dramatic turn.

God's promise is that I won't be consumed by evil or by circumstances beyond my control. This is the promise I cling to when we experience Christian's surgeries. It's the promise of God's steadfastness no matter what I'm experiencing that keeps my feet on solid ground. The world shakes and my circumstances bend, but I hold on to the truth that Jesus Christ is the same today, yesterday, and forever, amen. (See Hebrews 13:8.)

What does it mean that God doesn't change? I think it's simple: God is who He is and does not waver in His character. He is 100 percent good when our circumstances are not. Because He is unchanging, we can't look at Him through the lens of pain and think He has abandoned us. He hasn't. He is unmoving. When we think we're all alone, we're looking at Him from the wrong angle.

When the test says no cancer, He is good. And when the test comes back positive, He is still good.

God knows when our world is going to be shaken like a snow globe, leaving shards of hope falling around us. He's not surprised. And in those times He doesn't just help us survive; He helps us conquer. When we put our trust in Him, we don't come out of our hard times beaten and bloody. No, we come out triumphant because we have the ultimate victor on our side.

It's how we react to hard times that shows the world why we as followers of Christ are different. Instead of asking, "Why, God?," we have to be thankful that He's there and that He sees the end result. This doesn't mean that we pretend the situation isn't hard or we ignore the problems facing us. It just means we acknowledge an unchanging God and let Him lead us with grace through terrifying moments.

SEE GOD...

Even though our circumstances move us, they do not move God. What is going on in your life that makes you feel like your world is being shaken? Where do you see God in the midst of your storm?

_____

_____

God Is Unchanging

GIVE IT TO GOD IN PRAYER

Father, help me to trust You when my circumstances appear hopeless. Help me remember that I serve a God who does not bend to the winds but commands them to be still. You are my rock in times of need and my comfort in times of trouble. You are unchanging. Help me to always stay close to You. In Jesus's name, amen.

Day 9

LOOK BEYOND YOUR CIRCUMSTANCES

When you pass through the waters, I will be with you; and through the rivers, they shall not overwhelm you; when you walk through fire you shall not be burned, and the flame shall not consume you.
—Isaiah 43:2, ESV

IN THE MIDST of trouble it's hard to look beyond the situation.

When Christian was an infant, there was a period of time when we had zero answers, no diagnosis. His condition was so rare that even though we knew he was blind and had a cleft, we didn't know much else beyond that.

All I knew was the next thing—the next set of consent papers being shoved in our hands, the next meeting with a team of specialists, the next feeding session.

I was scared, angry, anxious, and worried. And I couldn't see beyond our circumstances.

We made each step in an exhausted state, praying we were making the right choices, feeling as if we were choking in the fog of bewilderment. Even as I prayed, I felt a spiritual block. I believed during my pregnancy that God was going to heal my son, and I felt like He totally failed me. While I mentally knew that God didn't *cause* Christian's disability, I spiritually felt further away from Him than ever before.

Psalm 25:10 says "All the paths of the Lord are steadfast love and faithfulness, for those who keep his covenant and his testimonies" (ESV). Wasn't I keeping His covenant? Hadn't I been a faithful servant? Then why did my path feel shaky?

My family's circumstances determined my relationship with my Savior. And as a result, I'd never felt more alone.

What I didn't know was that God was leading me through troubled waters because He needed to strengthen me as He guided me to the other side of our situation. I needed to grow as a person and in my faith. I don't believe God allowed Christian to have a birth defect solely for the purpose of making me stronger, but I believe God used our circumstances to refine me.

C. S. Lewis shares this sentiment beautifully.

> The more we believe that God hurts only to heal, the less we can believe that there is any use in begging for tenderness.... But suppose that what you are up against is a surgeon whose intentions are wholly good.... If he stopped before the operation was complete, all the pain up to that point would have been useless.
>
> But is it credible that such extremities of torture should be necessary for us? Well, take your choice. The tortures occur. If they are unnecessary, then there is no God or a bad one. If there is a good God, then these tortures are necessary. For no even moderately good Being could possibly inflict or permit them if they weren't.
>
> Either way, we're for it.[1]

There's comfort in knowing that God walks with us through our struggles. He promises in Isaiah 43:2 that we won't be burned when we walk through the fire, but sometimes I'd rather not walk through the fire at all.

Yet we have to look at the bigger picture, such as where we will end up after we've gone through the overwhelming rivers also spoken of in Isaiah 43:2. We'll end up closer to God and more confident than ever that our circumstances can't overwhelm us, because we serve a God who promises to keep us afloat.

SEE GOD...

What are some indications that God is with you during troubled times? How have you seen Him in the past? When you endure hardships, what are some of the feelings you have toward God? What does your spiritual walk look like?

_____

_____

_____

_____

_____

GIVE IT TO GOD IN PRAYER

Father, help keep my head above water. Please keep the road under my feet strong and sure. When I'm in the midst of trouble and heartache, keep my eyes focused on You so I can walk with grace and dignity. Let me be an example to others so that through all things You are given the praise. In Jesus's name, amen.

Day 10

QUESTIONING GOD

Then Gideon said to God, "Do not be angry with me, but let me speak just once more: Let me test, I pray, just once more with the fleece; let it now be dry only on the fleece, but on all the ground let there be dew." And God did so that night. It was dry on the fleece only, but there was dew on all the ground.
—JUDGES 6:39–40, NKJV

IS IT EVER OK to question God?

The Bible is full of people who did. David cried out to God. So did Abraham, Moses, the Israelites, Samson, and even Jesus. But the question begs, just because other people questioned Him, does that give us the right to do so as well?

I don't have the deep theological answer to that question, but during those early years with Christian I questioned God. I wanted to know why I felt isolated as I went through the toughest months of my life.

Questioning God

God is compassionate, and He is big enough to handle our questions. Most of all He understands our human condition and sympathizes with our hurt.

I often asked God, "Why me? Why my child?" God never leaned down to answer me, but He obviously didn't strike me dead for asking either. He was patient as I sorted through my emotions. Through His silence God allowed me to come to the conclusion that He was God and I was not.

It's crazy to look back and remember how important I thought I was, that the God of the universe should have to answer to me. My pain caused me to lose sight of the reality of God's supremacy and sovereignty. But instead of punishing me, God allowed me to struggle with my faith.

If you're a parent, you probably know what it's like when your kids ask you the same questions over and over. That's what we do to God, but unlike some of us, He never runs out of patience.

He can handle the big questions looming in our hearts. In fact, He already knows those questions exist before we ever speak them. He is compassionate when we hurt and gentle as we make sense of our pain. God may not answer us in the way we want Him to, but He definitely doesn't lose His cool with us when we ask big questions.

I wish my faith had been strong enough for me to

lean on God instead of questioning Him, but I honestly felt abandoned. I wanted to know why this was happening because it didn't seem fair.

Even though there are times when God allowed people to "get away with" asking Him questions, I think we should be careful about demanding answers from God. Gideon "fleeced" God three times, asking Him to confirm His word, but Gideon's motivation was pure. He had a huge decision to make that affected the lives of God's people. Gideon wanted to be absolutely sure the message he received was actually God's will. Gideon wasn't asking God to prove Himself based on a whim or a want.

When I questioned God, I did so because I felt abandoned, but I now realize that God never leaves us. I *know* that God was with me through the heartache; my problem was that I couldn't always *feel* Him.

It brings to mind the popular poem "Footprints." In it the author is walking along the beach with Jesus throughout his life. At the end he turns around and looks at his path. While he mostly sees two sets of footprints, there is only one set during the hardest parts of his life.

He questions Jesus about this, wondering aloud why Jesus left him alone. I love Jesus's answer. Jesus said, "During those times I carried you."

If you're wondering if God has left you alone to

make your own way through the pain your situation has caused, I can help you answer that question. He hasn't. He's with you. Always. Even if we don't feel like we're being carried, we are.

See God...

Do you think it's OK to question God? Have you ever done it before? If so, how did God answer you?

_____

_____

_____

_____

_____

Give It to God in Prayer

Father, thank You for being a personal God. Thank You for listening and hearing me. Father, when my heart is burdened with questions, help me remember that You are the ultimate answer to all my needs. In Jesus's name, amen.

Day 11

PUT YOUR TRUST IN GOD

Thus says the Lord, "Cursed is the man who trusts in mankind and makes flesh his strength, and whose heart turns away from the Lord."
— Jeremiah 17:5, nasb

Not fully trusting in God is always a mistake. Sometimes God uses people in our lives to teach us lessons or to confirm the path or direction we should take. For me, the people I felt I had to trust blindly were the doctors and specialists at the hospital. And I expected them to be perfect when it came to my child's care.

The thing is, people are always going to let us down. Only God will never fail us.

Because of this we need to show tons of grace to one another. And trust is something we build. Have you ever noticed that once someone really hurts you, it can take a long time for you to trust that person again?

That's because it takes time and intentional relationship-building to restore trust once it's broken.

Along with stories of great friendships in the Bible, there are many accounts of betrayal. Samson and Delilah, for instance. Or Judas, whose name has become synonymous with traitor.

Trust is such a special and fragile trait. It's easy to break and difficult to repair.

I want to be a trusted friend, daughter, and wife. I want people to know that I keep my word and won't cheat them, even when the odds are against me. I want to have friends who are the same way. Being trustworthy is a crucial quality to have, but the danger comes when we start putting the majority of our trust in other people or things instead of God.

We serve a righteously jealous God, and He makes it clear in Scripture that we are not to turn away from Him.

> Thus says the LORD: Cursed is the man who trusts in man and makes flesh his strength, and whose heart departs from the LORD.
> —JEREMIAH 17:5, MEV

I don't think God wants us to distrust everyone. We don't need a society full of suspicious, paranoid people (though some of us could stand to have our eyes opened a little to the dangers around us). But I think

God wants to make clear that He is the only One who can be trusted 100 percent.

Isaiah 2:22 says, "Don't put your trust in mere humans. They are as frail as breath. What good are they?" (NLT). When we put our trust in anyone but God, we are essentially trusting in things of our own making, things over which we have no control. When we trust in God, we know that He *is in* control and that with Him by our side we can bravely walk through whatever situation we face.

This is humbling for me. As a parent, my children trust in me completely. On their own they are helpless. Babies can't feed or clean themselves; they have zero access to resources apart from their parents, and they can't communicate what they want effectively.

I remember looking at my boys when they were infants and feeling an enormous amount of pressure to do everything I could for them. I wanted to be everything they needed. It's a strange instinct we have as parents to give our children everything they desire; it's a drive that we have to balance so they don't turn out to be spoiled or bratty.

Whether we're doing too much, too little, or just enough for them, our children don't know any better but to trust everything we do and say, especially when they're young like my boys are. But the sad reality is that no matter how hard we try to be perfect, we will make mistakes. And one day our children will realize that mommy and daddy aren't infallible. We're mere mortals.

We tell them that now, of course. If I make a mistake, I'll apologize and say I was wrong and ask for forgiveness. I do that because I want to show them humility and demonstrate a desire to always pursue a positive relationship.

But I also want them to know that God is different. He can *always* be trusted. He will never whisper the words, "Do you forgive Me?," because He will never hurt us. He hurts *with* us, and I think He is truly sorrowful that because of sin we will experience pain and heartache.

I think this is why He is so fierce when He declares in Scripture, "Stop trusting in mere humans, who have but a breath in their nostrils" (Isa. 2:22). He knows that trusting in our own or anyone else's strength will only lead to heartache. So with that in mind, I choose to make this my resolve: to be as honest and trustworthy as possible, to apologize sincerely when I mess up, and to fully trust God first and foremost. Always.

SEE GOD...

Have you ever placed your trust in yourself or someone else and ended up getting burned in the process? If so, describe what happened. How has God shown you that He alone is trustworthy?

_____

_____

_____

_____

_____

_____

_____

GIVE IT TO GOD IN PRAYER

I thank You, Father, that You are trustworthy. Teach me to demonstrate honesty and trustworthiness to everyone I meet. Help me to always put my trust in You instead of men, and teach me to give grace and mercy to others as You have shown to me. In Jesus's name, amen.

Day 12

MYSTERIOUS WAYS

*God will strengthen you with his own great
power so that you will not give up when
troubles come, but you will be patient.*
—Colossians 1:11, NCV

You've probably heard that the Lord works in mysterious ways. I think He sometimes speaks to us in unusual ways too.

One night while I was pregnant with Christian I turned on *60 Minutes* while I waited for Chris to get home. In that episode there was a report about a father who pushed his disabled son in races and marathons. Despite uneven terrain and long miles, they crossed the finish line again and again so that his son could experience life to the best of his ability.

At that point we had no idea that something was wrong with Christian, but I found myself boo-hooing until my nose hurt from blowing it so often. I like to blame my reaction on the pregnancy hormones, but I think there was more to it than that.

After watching that segment, I grabbed a piece of paper and penned a note to my unborn baby. It said in part, "You are my child and if something is wrong with you, nothing will change how much I love you."

Truer words were never spoken.

I had no idea why I felt led to write that note to my unborn baby, but I now believe God was using that moment to prepare me for what was to come.

I believe He does this more often than we think. God knows the end from the beginning (Isa. 46:10), but He's wise enough not to tell us the whole story of our lives. We might not mind the ending, but I'm sure we wouldn't want to go through the dark, winding roads and deep valleys that await us along the way. I know I didn't.

God may not tell us what is to come, but that doesn't mean He doesn't prepare us and give us strength beforehand.

Think of Moses. God's plan was to deliver the people of Israel from bondage in Egypt, so He "gifted" Pharaoh's daughter with an Israelite infant. How brilliant to plant an insider right smack-dab in the middle of the royal court! Moses grew up Egyptian, yet God used him to stand up and fight for his true people.

Mysterious Ways

God's plan was for Moses to lead his people out of Egypt to freedom. But God had to take Moses out of Egypt to prepare him to accomplish that task.

The Moses who fled Egypt after killing an Egyptian taskmaster and the one who returned forty years later were pretty different. Among the many things God did during Moses's time in the wilderness was use it as a training ground to prepare him to be the kind of leader He had called him to be. God humbled Moses so he wouldn't rely on his own strength but on God's.

The Lord does the same for us. He prepares us through circumstances to teach us to trust Him, to believe that He will work all things together for our good, to lean on Him when we don't know what to do, to trust that He's good no matter how bad the situation looks, to know that He will never leave us or forsake us.

While watching that episode of *60 Minutes*, the Lord opened my heart to the courageous way a person could parent a child with a disability. I didn't know at the time that I would benefit from that father's example to enrich my child's life with fun, adventure, and new experiences, but I have.

God was preparing me. Some people may dismiss my reaction to the *60 Minutes* segment as coincidence, but I know it was the Holy Spirit's way of readying my heart for the journey we've traveled.

When you find yourself in the middle of adversity, it's easy to think you're in over your head or that you can't handle the road before you. But nothing surprises God. In big and small ways He provides the strength you'll need, whether you recognize it or not, so you won't give up when troubles come.

SEE GOD...

They say hindsight is 20/20. Think back on a difficult season in your life. What are some ways you now see that God prepared you, giving you strength, building your faith, and growing your confidence in Him?

_____

_____

_____

_____

_____

_____

GIVE IT TO GOD IN PRAYER

Father, You know all things, and You give me the strength to handle the things that I have no idea are even coming. You help me grow in You. You build my faith. You remind me of Your ever-present help. And You are always with me. Thank You for never leaving me to walk the hard roads on my own. In Jesus's name, amen.

Day 13

YOU ARE AWESOME

For we are God's masterpiece. He has created us anew in Christ Jesus, so we can do the good things he planned for us long ago.
—Ephesians 2:10, NLT

Y OU ARE FEARFULLY and wonderfully made. I am fearfully and wonderfully made.

Those words are written as clear as day in Psalm 139:14, but it can be hard to really believe them.

When I held Christian for the first time, I looked past his features and thought about who he was. And I knew that despite Christian's disabilities, God had an incredible plan for my son's life, a plan that has included a storehouse of blessings and a journey of mischievous, fun-loving, rough-and-tumble escapades.

It's easier for me to look as an outsider into someone's world and say, "Yes, God has great plans for her. She can do *x, y, and z*." Or I can see how God can use someone's different-ness as a platform to bring

Him glory. That's how I see Christian's life. People can *and have* come to know God because of my sweet five-year-old boy's journey.

But I find it hard to look at my own life and see the good plans God has. If I were to share some of the negative self-talk I've beaten myself down with over the years, you may be horrified. I'm sure God hates it when I tear into myself or beat myself up. If I'm His creation, His handiwork, His masterpiece, then my negativity is an affront to Him.

When doubts or negativity come to mind, I have to stop them immediately. God doesn't see any of us as worthless; He sees us as valuable. He has given you and me special qualities to fulfill a purpose in our lives and in the world. We have to hold on to what makes us unique so we can be used by God in the special way He created us to be used.

I don't think people say this enough, but God thinks you are incredible. If we could see ourselves through His eyes, even for a split second, we wouldn't be able to handle all the love we would see there.

When I became a parent, I understood God in a whole new way. I understood what it meant to love someone so much that you can't breathe for thinking about it, how you memorize every inch of their face, their body, their sounds, their movements, their breaths.

It's a love so different from the love I understood when I got married. The love between spouses is a love that reflects how God loves His church, His bride. The love of a parent reflects the love of the Father to His child, and it's bigger than any word can express.

God loves you. You are His masterpiece.

Author Lori Roeleveld puts it this way: "That's the purpose of all art—to be so beautiful, so provocative, so mesmerizing that we remember the glory of our Creator as if roused from our nap amid the poppies and recalled to our purpose and our journey."[1]

Regardless of your situation in life, how many friends you have, how you spend your time, the amount of money sitting in the bank, the type of car parked in your driveway, or the size of the bills stacked on the kitchen table, God thinks you're awesome. And He has a plan for you. You are His masterpiece, and He wants your life to be seen for His glory.

SEE GOD...

List five characteristics that make you special. Reflect on them, and describe how you have been uniquely created. What does your list show you about your purpose?

_____

_____

_____

_____

_____

_____

_____

_____

_____

GIVE IT TO GOD IN PRAYER

Father, how incredible is it that the One who hung the stars in the sky sees me as His child and loves me as a good Father would. Thank You for loving me despite my faults and for calling me Yours. Help me to always remember how much You love me! In Jesus's name, amen.

Day 14

SACRIFICE TAKES MANY FORMS

If you love those who love you, what credit is that to you? Even sinners love those who love them. And if you do good to those who are good to you, what credit is that to you? Even sinners do that.
—Luke 6:32–33

Having children means making sacrifices—a lot of them. Parents sacrifice money, time, a spotless home, and daily showers. You get my drift.

People often say that becoming a parent makes you grow up, and that is totally true. Even when you're married, you're still, at the root of it, two semi-selfish people looking out for your collective best interests. When you throw a helpless, innocent newborn into the mix, everything changes.

There is this feeling that overwhelms you. You'd give

your right arm, literally, to make sure that baby has everything he needs. There are very few things on the "I Would Not Do This to Feed My Child" list, and I know that in my heart of hearts I'd fight to the death to protect my babies. We see this type of "Mama Bear" behavior in nature, but I never fully expected it to happen to me. Until it did.

I look back at the amount of time, energy, resources, money, and relationships that I've sacrificed to put my family first. I don't regret any of it, although there were times when I felt as if my body would give out and I didn't know where my next source of relief would come from. We sacrifice for those we love, but God tells us to sacrifice also for those we don't.

What we do for those we love we need to do for others, even those who are rude and hateful to us. Scripture says in Luke 6:29–31, "If someone slaps you on one cheek, turn to them the other also. If someone takes your coat, do not withhold your shirt from them. Give to everyone who asks you, and if anyone takes what belongs to you, do not demand it back. Do to others as you would have them do to you."

Overall people's reactions to Christian have taken a complete 180-degree turnaround, but I dealt with ignorance and hatred. People have stared and made rude comments, and some have even claimed it would have been more loving of me to have aborted him. Over time

I've developed a thicker skin, but my heart can never fully block the evil spoken about my child or my decision to let him live.

Those are the people God demands that I help. Yet my human side screams out to God, "How can You ask this of me? There are people who threaten to light my son on fire, to gouge him and violate him, and I'm supposed to *sacrifice* for them?"

The soft answer I hear back from God in my soul is, "Yes, because I 'presented Christ as a sacrifice of atonement, through the shedding of his blood—to be received by faith'" (Rom. 3:25).

If we claim to be followers of Jesus, we can't only love the people who love us. The verse in Luke says that even sinners, aka nonbelievers, do that. Who doesn't adore the person who adores us back?

The Bible says we have to love everyone, even those who hurt our feelings, who are insensitive, or who make threats against us.

I easily understand this concept of loving those who love me. I am blessed to have an amazing Facebook community. The support and love my family receives is overwhelming and truly makes me feel like we have a village behind us. I appreciate you guys so much.

I have to work on loving the people who don't love me. If I choose to show love only to my family, my friends, and my community of supporters, I'm no better than "a sinner." It's choosing to sacrifice the pride and ego, the knowledge that I'm right, and my weak human spirit that allows God to shine through.

Only God can give us the strength we need to make the sacrifices that are required of us each day. Only He can strengthen us to get through the obstacles we face. And only He can help us love those who aren't always easy to like. But when we choose to get out of the way and let Him lead, He can accomplish this and so much more through us.

SEE GOD...

In what areas of your life do you have people who are difficult to love? How can you specifically sacrifice your pride to love them? In what ways do you see God working through your sacrifice?

_____

_____

_____

_____

_____

_____

Give It to God in Prayer

Father, let me always remember that this life is all about Jesus Christ. My purpose is to bring You glory in all I do. Through the highs and lows, the good times and bad, help me keep my eyes fixed on Jesus, the author and perfecter of my faith. Give me ears to hear You, eyes to see You, and a heart that is receptive to You. Wherever You lead me, whatever You call me to do, however You see fit to guide my steps, let me always be pleasing to You. In Jesus's name, amen.

Day 15

HOLDING FAST TO GOD'S PROMISES

Everyone then who hears these words of mine and does them will be like a wise man who built his house on the rock. And the rain fell, and the floods came, and the winds blew and beat on that house, but it did not fall, because it had been founded on the rock. And everyone who hears these words of mine and does not do them will be like a foolish man who built his house on the sand. And the rain fell, and the floods came, and the winds blew and beat against that house, and it fell, and great was the fall of it.
—Matthew 7:24–27, esv

I DON'T KNOW HOW I would have survived the last few years if I didn't have God. Truly. Life almost broke me as it was. If it wasn't for my friend inviting me to church when I was a teenager and my decision to accept Jesus as my Lord and Savior, my whole world would be in darkness. I'm so thankful for the foundation in Jesus that started way before I found myself in a position where I only got out of bed in the morning through His strength.

Without God, what would I have done?

What would I have become?

What life would my family have?

It's hard to even imagine.

Church became an integral part of my calendar after becoming a Christian. I met friends through youth group and found others in college who shared my beliefs. I met and married a man who put his faith in Jesus. We got baptized on the same day, and that's such a special memory and experience that we share.

A lesson that is deeply ingrained in my heart is that during the good days, the *easy* days, we have to create the foundation, figuratively building houses of faith. Each verse that we memorize and apply to our lives is a like a brick carefully laid in place.

When the storm winds come (or the Big, Bad Wolf if fairy tales are your thing), we can hide out in the spiritual houses we've built with God's Word, drawing comfort from the God who loves us and protects us. What's more, we serve a God who tells us ahead of time that the tempest is coming. He warns us to be ready, and we have to choose if we want to be wise.

In those first years after Christian was born, I hoped that maybe, just maybe, God really was who He said He was and that He would do what He said he would do. The Bible says in Hebrews 11:1 that faith is the substance of things hoped for, the evidence of things not seen. Because I knew that God had promised me life—life to the full (see John 10:10)—there was a tiny part of me that held on to the hope that life would get better, even when it looked like everything I had believed was a lie.

I had to rely on the foundation of truth found in Scripture: that God loved me and that His plans for Christian and me were part of a prosperous hope and future.

Honestly I had nothing else to hold on to but those truths. I was powerless to heal my child, to fix our situation, to change the circumstances. But what I could do was hope that God would keep His promises to me.

He did, and still does.

We grow through the trials and hard times. Our faith is strengthened through circumstances. During the peaceful times we must devour God's Word with the same hunger we have when life feels desperate. That's how we build a foundation strong enough to withstand the storms.

Although God certainly didn't fulfill His promises in the ways I expected Him to or thought He should, again and again He has proved Himself faithful. God gave us Scripture as a solid foundation, and every time He proves Himself to us, the walls of our proverbial faith house grow taller and stronger.

SEE GOD...

How has God helped you in times of trouble? What are you doing to build a strong foundation in your life to prepare for life's storms? Describe a situation during which God sheltered you when life became difficult.

___

___

___

___

GIVE IT TO GOD IN PRAYER

Father, help me to build my foundation on the rock of Jesus Christ. Send me people, circumstances, and scriptures that will help me build up and strengthen my foundation in You. Help me to remember that when the storms come, I have Your Word to lean on, for You are my Rock and my Redeemer. In Jesus's name, amen.

Day 16

RIBBONS OF PRAYER

Speak to the sons of Israel, and tell them that they shall make for themselves tassels on the corners of their garments throughout their generations, and that they shall put on the tassel of each corner a cord of blue. It shall be a tassel for you to look at and remember all the commandments of the Lord.
—Numbers 15:38–39, nasb

Before each of Christian's surgeries we offer our Facebook and blog community the opportunity to send in prayer ribbons. This tradition started after I received a care package from Cranio Care Bears. They are a sweet company started by two moms whose sons were both diagnosed with craniosynostosis, a rare skull disorder.

During one of our multiple doctors' appointments Christian had been diagnosed with craniosynostosis, a diagnosis that I disagreed with. After a ton of research and second-, third-, and fourth-opinion appointments with other specialists, we were relieved to find out that our little one did *not* have this condition and would not have to undergo a frightening neurosurgery.

Considering the fact that Christian did not have this rare birth disorder, I was surprised when the care package showed up. Many people have sent gifts to Christian over the years, so I thanked God silently for the giver of the gift, and now publicly say thank you to this individual, as well as everyone who has shown kindness to our family in the form of gifts and prayers.

Inside the box were a ton of goodies—socks, toiletries, baby toys—but what really caught my eye were the beautiful ribbons. Each one had an affirmation or message of hope written on them. This inspired us to ask our friends and family to write a prayer on a six-inch piece of ribbon for Christian's first surgery, and we looped them together to form a chain.

With that a tradition was born.

Through the years people have become extremely creative with the ribbons. One ribbon that really sticks out to me is full of bright colors with several tactile things for Christian to touch. Each individual button and strip of fringe had been carefully hand-sewn. The level of detail is incredible; the person who created it obviously put a lot of thought and time into the design.

Christian understands the purpose of the ribbon,

and he runs the strands through his fingers while we whisper prayers before he is admitted to the preoperative areas. Once he's been led away from me, the prayer ribbon is placed in my lap, and I weep into the fabric.

When I cry and pray while holding the prayer ribbon, I am always reminded that God's grace is sufficient and He did not leave me here alone.

Having a tangible or physical reminder of God's presence and love isn't a new idea. Some people use prayer beads or a rosary when they pray. When Christian is in surgery, I run my fingers over the ribbons people have sent and prayed over. The Jewish people used, and still use, the *tzitzit* (pronounced tsēt-'sēt).

The *tzitzit* are tassels found at the end or edge of the Jewish prayer shawl, which is called a tallit. We see throughout Scripture this physical evidence of God's love and His promise to take care of His people.

Zechariah 8:23 says, "Thus says the LORD of hosts, 'In those days ten men from all the nations will grasp the garment of a Jew, saying, "Let us go with you, for we have heard that God is with you"'" (NASB). In Luke 8:43–44 a woman who is suffering from excessive bleeding reaches through the crowd to touch the *tzitzit*, the fringes of Jesus's tallit, to be healed.

In 1 Samuel 24 David was hiding from King Saul in a cave. Saul had to relieve himself and used the exact cave where David was hiding. David had the chance to kill him, but instead, David snuck up behind Saul and did something worse. He cut off the fringes of Saul's tallit, the *tzitzit*. This act would have humiliated Saul because his *tzitzit* represented his God-given authority.

We serve a God who understands that we love Him and want to be near Him, even though we can't see Him. That's why He gave the Jewish people the *tzitzit* as a physical reminder of His presence in their lives. And I believe that's why He gave me the prayer ribbon—not only so I can remember that people all across the country are praying for Christian, but also so I can remember that I serve a big God who is in complete control of the future, both mine and Christian's.

SEE GOD...

Some people take the idea of using a physical object to connect them to God much too far. They think the item is what draws them close to the Father, and nothing could be further from the truth. In His kindness God gives us physical reminders of His presence with us. But He is always with us, and we will feel closer to Him as we spend time praying, reading the Bible, or worshipping Him. What do you do to draw close to God and sense His presence? When you don't feel Him, what helps you remember that God is still with you? What do you think God meant when He said in Hebrews 13:5 that He would never leave us nor forsake us?

_____

_____

_____

_____

Give It to God in Prayer

Dear God, I know that You are powerful and present. You are not a God who is too busy for me or one who does not care. Your love for me is so steadfast that You sent Jesus as the Great High Priest who is able to sympathize with our weakness. Because of Jesus I can confidently approach Your throne and receive mercy and grace. Help me to draw closer to You each day, Father, and to know that You are always near me. Sometimes it may not feel like it's true, but I know that You will never leave me. I give You thanks, Lord, that You are always in my midst. In Jesus's name, amen.

Day 17

LETTING GO AND LETTING GOD

Three times I pleaded with the Lord about this, that it should leave me. But he said to me, "My grace is sufficient for you, for my power is made perfect in weakness." Therefore I will boast all the more gladly of my weaknesses, so that the power of Christ may rest upon me.
—2 Corinthians 12:8–9, esv

Sometimes we trust God only when we feel we have no other choice. We've covered all the options on our own; now it's time to let God lead the way.

I never feel this is as strongly as when a nurse comes into the waiting area to take Christian to the preoperative room. The nurse is always kind. Her expression is sweet, but I know my face in comparison is fearful and apprehensive.

I use those last few precious seconds to squeeze Christian as hard as I can, kiss his face, and tell him I love him, that he's so brave.

I stifle sobs, my arms outstretched as Christian is transferred from the security of my arms to the care of hers. My fingers keep hold of Christian as long as possible, but eventually he's out of my reach.

In that moment I am unashamedly standing with my arms up, my palms facing the heavens. I've surrendered one of the most precious gifts God has given me, but in those moments I am more aware than ever that Christian isn't truly mine. He is completely and totally God's.

There is a sketch floating around social media of a little girl holding a teddy bear in her arms. Jesus kneels in front of her with a much larger version of the same teddy bear behind His back. He asks her to trust Him by letting go of the teddy bear.

She looks up at him and says, "…but I love it."

Sometimes we are that little girl. Our fingers grip whatever treasure we can hold on to for fear that we either won't get anything better or we'll end up with nothing at all.

The truth is, when we let go fully, when we open our hands, we put ourselves in a posture of receiving. We let go so we can "let God." We can't be afraid to let what we love out of our grip because even though we believe we own everything, we truly don't control anything.

Do something with me, right now. No matter where you are while you're reading this, open your fingers and turn your palm toward the sky. Hold that position for a moment.

Take a deep breath and let go of the frustration you're feeling. Ask God to replace any stress with peace.

Our God is strong in our weakness, and our outstretched hands symbolize our surrender to His holiness and grace. By taking this posture—not just physically but in our hearts—we allow Him to remove our troubles and set us on solid ground.

SEE GOD...

What are you holding on to that you need to let go of? Are there areas of your life that you feel you have to stay on top of or keep control?

_____

_____

_____

_____

_____

_____

Give It to God in Prayer

Father, help me let go of what I hold on to. Allow me to have an open spirit so I can receive Your mercy, kindness, and blessings. You are the Father who loves to give His children good things. Help me not miss out because I'm focused on keeping what I already have. In Jesus's name, amen.

Day 18

HOLY BOLDNESS

In all these things we are more than conquerors through Him who loved us.
—ROMANS 8:37, MEV

I ALWAYS THOUGHT I was a confident person until I was tested. Turns out, I'm only confident in what I know. Put me in a situation where I'm out of my comfort zone or haven't done enough research, and my stomach feels like a big puddle of soup.

When Christian was little, most of my prayers were about his healing. I asked God to watch over my baby, to protect him, to give him rest and comfort and peace. I didn't realize that God was quietly working in my heart as well.

Trusting doctors and hospital staff seemed like the right thing to do, until a nagging sensation would flutter inside me. Sometimes I'd ignore it, and then I'd notice something in Christian that only a parent would notice. Because I *knew* my child, I sensed things, and began to learn to trust my instincts.

There is no real explanation for this "mother's intuition," but any parent who has experienced it knows exactly what I'm talking about. It's a fine balance, really, learning to be bold without burning any bridges. After all, we still needed those doctors, even if they made a mistake in their assessment of Christian.

Eventually I learned to trust this instinct, but I believe it was more than just my mommy brain on overdrive. I believe the Holy Spirit was prompting me to look further, to stand up for what I knew to be right.

I also had to learn that when I speak up, someone somewhere will disagree. Online there are people who get angry because I share photos of Christian. In hospital settings there have been doctors who refused to listen to alternative opinions.

Through this process I learned to care less about pleasing people and more about pleasing God. It's been extremely hard to break my people-pleasing nature, but God has done a miraculous work in me. Sometimes people aren't going to like the choices I make, but I don't answer to them. I answer to my heavenly Father.

It is this confidence being cultivated in my spirit that I want to overflow into all areas of my life. I want a holy boldness, the guts to stand up for the truth of God's Word.

I love that the Bible says in Romans 8:37 that we are more than conquerors. To be a conqueror is to be victorious over an adversary, but to be more than a conqueror is to be overwhelmingly victorious. It means the opposition doesn't stand a chance.

We are victors. Because of Jesus's sacrifice, we serve a God who has overcome the world (John 16:33). As the apostle Paul asks in Romans 8:31, if God is for us, who can be against us?

What a powerful truth. The God of all creation is on our side. We can be completely confident because we serve an omnipresent, all-knowing God who not only loves us and wants us to succeed but who has also already won the spiritual battle over sin, hell, and death. There is literally no one and nothing that can take Him down.

So easily we forget what kind of power we wield. God is our ever-present help in trouble (Ps. 46:1). The Holy Spirit is inside of us. We have a Savior who died to defeat sin and death and give us personal access to the God who created the universe. So often, though, we walk about as if that isn't the truth.

If we truly lived with this type of confidence, think about the amount of worrying we could toss aside. Our anxiety levels would decrease. Our happy hormones would fill our bodies, and we'd radiate joy. I wish I carried myself with that confidence every day, but truth be told, I have days when I struggle with it as well. During those times I have to run to God and let Him remind me who He is and who He says I am.

The Bible is a constant reminder of who we are and whose we are. It's so important to dive in to God's Word and get those pep talks that can give us the confidence to carry ourselves like the children of God. He created us, called us, and equipped us in our lives, and *nothing* can separate us from His love, not even our own shortcomings and failings. When challenges present themselves in our lives, we can have confidence, a holy boldness in the Father who stands with us. In Him, we are more than conquerors.

SEE GOD...

On a scale of one to ten, how would you rate your confidence level? What three areas of your life do you feel the most confident in? In what three areas do you wish you felt more confident? How has God increased your confidence through the years?

_____

_____

_____

GIVE IT TO GOD IN PRAYER

Father, help me to remember that no matter the challenges I'm facing in life, You are behind me. You are with me. I can do all things through Your strength. You are my confidence. Please give me holy boldness so I can worry less and trust You more. In Jesus's name, amen.

Day 19

TRAIN-WRECK MOMENTS

I love you, O LORD, my strength. The LORD is my rock and my fortress and my deliverer, my God, my rock, in whom I take refuge, my shield, and the horn of my salvation, my stronghold.
—PSALM 18:1–2, ESV

I ALWAYS TRIED TO be strong during Christian's surgeries. Anyone who has had a loved one go through a major procedure knows how stressful and helpless-feeling it can be. For Christian's most major surgery I found myself vomiting in the family-sized restroom, tears and snot running down my face. This was not the Lacey I show on Facebook or the strong mom I had to be at his doctor appointments. My child's life—his future—would be completely out of my hands for the next eight hours. I realized only God knew what would happen, and I broke down.

When I emerged from the restroom, my face was tear-stained, but I took a few deep breaths and braved the quizzical looks from my family. I sat in the stiff waiting room chair and engaged in small talk, but my mind was on my baby boy, and my heart was praying for healing.

Surgeries aren't the only time that I find myself not trusting God the way I should, though. When the electric bill is larger than I think it should be or we're fighting with the insurance company, I take on the weight of having to make everything perfect.

But we don't live in a perfect world, and I'm not supermom.

When I try to be the rock of the family during hard times, I end up becoming overstressed and overtired. I have to rely on God.

There is an amazing quote from author Lisa Bevere that sort of sums up how we can give ourselves a break: "If you think you've blown God's plan for your life, rest in this: You, my beautiful friend, are not that powerful."[1]

I love that.

I'm not that powerful.

I'm not perfect.

Thankfully God doesn't call us to be any of those things. He calls us to trust Him.

God has a plan for me. He has a plan for my family.

He has a plan for you too, and while we may step off the path sometimes or get derailed, we know that God can get us back on track. Instead of trying to keep the train of life moving on my own, I need to let God take over. He is the rock. He is the stronghold. He is the refuge.

Interestingly God is only able to work in us when we surrender to Him. It's almost a daily acknowledging that He is in control. When I let my guard down and admit my weakness, God stretches out His arms and allows me to rest in His strength.

We're going to have train-wreck moments in our life, but God is our ever-present help in times of trouble (Ps. 46:1). We have to be willing to accept His assistance.

SEE GOD...

Think about a train-wreck moment in your life. Did you find it hard to trust God? What keeps you from leaning on God first? Do you try to take care of life's obstacles on your own? If so, what can you do to change that tendency?

_____

_____

_____

Give It to God in Prayer

Father, I am only made strong in my weakness. Please help me surrender to Your will and be willing to be made less so You can receive the praise and glory for the good works that You do. You are my ever-present help in time of trouble, and I praise and thank You for caring for me so deeply. In Jesus's name, amen.

Day 20

WHEN GOD ALLOWS THE PAIN

But he was pierced for our transgressions; he was crushed for our iniquities; upon him was the chastisement that brought us peace, and with his wounds we are healed.
—Isaiah 53:5, ESV

I ONCE HEARD A story about a pastor whose son was diagnosed with cancer. As he sat with his son in the hospital one night after a surgical procedure, the pastor wished, just like I did with Christian, that he could experience the pain instead of his little boy.

But God used that experience to help him realize that the pain was part of his son's healing process. He had to endure it in order to get better.

In that moment the pastor also realized something profound about God. He's a good Father—the best, in fact—and He doesn't like to see us in pain either. But He knows there are some kinds of pain that we have to go through because it's part of the process that will make us better. The pain is a necessary part of the journey.

As a parent I wished Christian didn't have to go through the pain of surgeries at only a few days old (or ever). I would take all of it from him if I could. No one wants to watch their child hurt or suffer, but we live in a fallen world. When unpleasant moments happen, God doesn't simply remove the pain. But the good news is that He doesn't remove Himself either. He stands with us, holds us close, and allows us to feel His presence and know that He is near.

It's easy to get mad at God when He allows pain or suffering. I'm never thankful for the refining fire when I'm standing in the midst of the blaze. I'm sure Shadrach, Meshach, and Abednego would have preferred to avoid the fiery furnace too. But God chose not to keep them from the fire; He stood with them through the heat and made sure the flames didn't destroy them. (See Daniel 3.)

That's what God does for us. He stands with us in those painful moments and uses them to help mold us into who we are called to be. He shapes us to be more like Jesus.

One of the amazing things about our God is that He understands exactly how we feel when we're in pain. Jesus loves us and wants us to be whole, so He endured the ultimate pain—both physical and spiritual—in our place. When we think about what Jesus went through on our behalf, it puts the pain we experience on Earth in perspective.

The prophet Isaiah said Jesus was pierced for our transgressions and crushed for our iniquities; the chastisement that brought us peace was upon Him, and with His wounds we are healed (Isa. 53:5). That's pretty incredible if you stop to really think about it. We are healed through His suffering.

God the Father had to let Jesus, His Son, experience the pain of the cross, because it was the only way we could experience salvation, healing, and wholeness. It was a necessary part of the process.

God hurts to see us hurt, so when He allows pain in our lives, we can always rest assured that it's not because He loves us any less. The pain has a purpose.

We often think of physical pain when we talk about being hurt, but heartbreak can be crushing as well. Depression can set in, and we can feel far away from God emotionally. Our feelings can be fragile, and sometimes God lets us walk through emotional hardships.

Sometimes, in time, we are able to see what God saw all along, why He allowed certain legs of our journey to be marked with suffering. But there are other things that we may never understand. In those times we must see our pain through eyes of faith and remind ourselves that God always has our best interest at heart. And just as He did for Shadrach, Meshach, and Abednego, He will see us through.

See God...

What has been the most painful experience in your life so far? Was it personal pain, or was it experiencing someone else's pain? How did God see you through that journey?

_____

_____

_____

_____

Give It to God in Prayer

Father, sometimes life can be difficult, and there are times when I'm hurt physically, and there are times when my heart is broken. In those times remind me that You are near to the brokenhearted and that You will never leave me or forsake me. When the storms of life come and the fires of refinement burn, lead me closer to You. In Jesus's name, amen.

Day 21

QUIET FAITH

> *When Daniel knew that the document had been signed, he went to his house where he had windows in his upper chamber open toward Jerusalem. He got down on his knees three times a day and prayed and gave thanks before his God, as he had done previously.*
> —Daniel 6:10, ESV

GOD MADE US all with different personalities. Some of us are extroverts and feel alive when we're around people. Some of us are introverts and feel recharged when we are by ourselves. Similarly some of us are outgoing, and some of us are more reserved.

There's nothing wrong with having different personality types. I believe we're all a reflection of God. He created us in His image, and we each have different aspects of God's personality in various amounts.

Sometimes, though, it can feel like having a quiet faith is a negative thing.

Loud faith gets a lot of attention. We see people praising God with hands raised high in the air, proclaiming the goodness and power of God during prayers. Those of us who are quieter can feel like we get overlooked or are thought of as "less holy" when we don't do the same thing. (Then we feel this little burst of guilt for even being concerned about it.)

Honestly sometimes it can seem that those with a quiet faith aren't really sold out for God. But we see in Scripture that quiet faith can be powerful.

One such example is found in Daniel 6:10: "Now when Daniel learned that the decree had been published, he went home to his upstairs room where the windows opened toward Jerusalem. Three times a day he got down on his knees and prayed, giving thanks to his God, just as he had done before."

Daniel was close to King Darius. He was a trusted adviser, which naturally made the other government leaders jealous. It took some plotting, because Daniel was such an upstanding guy, but they figured out a way to use Daniel's faith against him. The jealous men told King Darius that it should be against the law for anyone to pray to anyone but the king, and he agreed.

This is a great example of how a person's ego can get the best of him and hurt others. King Darius sealed the

Quiet Faith

law with his signet ring. And once the law went into effect, all the wicked men had to do was wait. They knew Daniel prayed, like clockwork, in his room three times a day to the God of Abraham. So it was just a matter of time before Daniel would disobey the law.

Daniel, being a government official, was certainly aware of the king's edict. But we see no evidence that he held a rally or staged a public protest. He simply prayed in his room, near the window as always. There were no shouting matches or billboards—just quiet faithfulness to his God.

To think Daniel was fearless in this takes away his humanity—I'm sure he was scared, but he knew that God would only bless his obedience. He knew he was doing the right thing.

I wonder if Daniel considered that God might not save him from the consequences of his actions. After all, the king declared that those who violated this law would be thrown in a den of lions. They kept those lions hungry, so that was capital punishment, in case you were wondering.

I love the fact that Daniel's decision to be faithful wasn't contingent on the outcome he would experience. He didn't need God to promise Him beforehand that he'd come out of the lions' den unscathed. He considered his commitment to spend time with God in prayer three times each day more important than any threat from the king or his wicked officials. And he was willing to face the outcome.

Here's another thing I love about this story. God met Daniel's quiet faith with a loud, dynamic response. When Daniel was punished by being thrown into a den of lions, God sent an angel to close the lions' mouths. After the king tossed and turned the entire night, worried about the way his law impacted Daniel, he ran to the lions' den and called out for Daniel, saying, "Daniel, servant of the living God, has your God whom you serve continually been able to deliver you from the lions?" (Dan. 6:20, MEV).

The king hoped Daniel's God had saved him. And He had.

Daniel's faith was quiet but consistent, and in the end the king and all the government officials were made aware of the incredible power of God.

It's not common practice today for people to be thrown into lions' dens for praying to God, but sometimes it feels like we're staring into the open mouth of an enemy. We can feel like God isn't going to come through, but what we see as the end of the story, God may see as an opportunity to show Himself strong on our behalf.

It's not guaranteed that God will always save us in such a miraculous way as He did Daniel; after all, Christians are martyred around the world every day. But we must never forget that we serve the same God who saved Daniel. And when we choose to be faithful to Him, we can trust that He'll be with us, no matter what.

SEE GOD...

Do you think you have loud or quiet faith? What are some of the consistent ways you live out your faith?

_____

_____

_____

_____

_____

GIVE IT TO GOD IN PRAYER

Father, You created us in Your image. I praise You for You are wonderful. Thank You for being the God who saves, and thank You for creating me to be the way I am. Please help me always to do the right thing when it comes to praising and honoring You. In Jesus's name, amen.

Day 22

WEEPING INTO JOY

You turned my wailing into dancing; you removed my sackcloth and clothed me with joy, that my heart may sing your praises and not be silent. Lord my God, I will praise you forever.
—Psalm 30:11–12

I've cried in the front seat of my car more times than I can count—after ultrasounds, on the way home after leaving my newborn in the hospital's NICU, after dealing with rude comments and stares in public, after a tiring day on the way home from law school. It seems that tears became a therapeutic method of dealing with frustration, sadness, and heartache.

As Christian grew older, being in public became difficult. I've never been one to want any attention, but it felt like a spotlight followed us everywhere we went. I knew Christian was too young to be aware of what was happening, but my heart broke for the day when

Weeping Into Joy

my little boy would become self-conscious and cognizant of the whispers, laughs, and cruelty.

After the YouTube video of Christian's story went viral, we were contacted by several media outlets, even major ones like *The Doctors* TV show. Through that exposure people in our town saw the behind-the-scenes reality, and God allowed a major switch to be flipped.

Today when we go to the store or have a family outing, it still feels like a spotlight is on us, but now it's positive. People recognize Christian. They talk *to* him instead of *about* him. The people who keep up with our Facebook page will ask about recent events. They take photos with us and are genuinely excited to have "spotted us" in our small town.

Even the tone of our social media experiences has changed. The majority of comments are positive encouragements, although I still deal with people who think I have a monster for a son and that I must cry myself to sleep every night. (Yes, I've heard that and worse.)

God turned my tears of heartache into tears of joy. He exchanged my pain for gladness, my weeping for a fullness of life that I didn't even know was possible. When Christian was just a few days old, I didn't know if he would survive a major surgery. Now I watch in amazement as he marvels at the wind brushing his cheeks and the sounds of leaves crackling under his feet.

He loves to be snuggled, loves to be tickled, and loves to be loved. His laugh is infectious. At one time in my life I could hardly imagine the Christian I know today.

As David wrote in Psalm 30, God turned my wailing into dancing; He clothed me with joy, that my heart may sing His praises and not be silent.

Psalm 30 is such a beautiful psalm of praise. I love how David bares his soul to the Lord. He admits that he cried out to God for help, cried out for mercy, and God answered him. David didn't care if people viewed his dependence as a sign of weakness. He refused to do anything but give God the praise and honor He so richly deserves.

That's the type of attitude I want to have in my heart at all times.

God isn't intimidated by our tears. Ecclesiastes 3:4 says there is a time to mourn. Even our Savior cried at least three times that are documented in Scripture: John 11:35 when He heard that Lazarus had died, in Luke 19:41 when He wept over the city of Jerusalem, and in Hebrews 5:7 when Jesus was in the Garden of Gethsemane.

When life doesn't go our way or our feelings are hurt, our God understands. But He doesn't leave us alone in our sadness. He beckons with arms open wide.

SEE GOD...

Think about the last time you had a really good, soul-cleansing cry. How did you feel afterward? Are there times in your life when you felt in your spirit that God was lifting you up and comforting your heartache? Describe that experience.

_____

_____

_____

_____

_____

_____

GIVE IT TO GOD IN PRAYER

Father, I praise You for turning my weeping into joy and my mourning into dancing. Lord, may Your praise always flow from my mouth. Help me to remember that weeping may last for the night but joy comes in the morning. In Jesus's name, amen.

Day 23

OUR EVER-PRESENT HELP

God is our refuge and strength, an ever-present help in trouble.
—Psalm 46:1

There were times during our search for a plastic surgeon when I felt completely helpless and alone. I didn't know who to reach out to, and I didn't know how to ask for help. As a way of relieving some of the stress, I blogged. This wasn't a natural response for me. In fact, it was a kind NICU social worker who suggested I start writing about our experiences.

I'm so glad I did.

Through the blog I was able to express myself in ways that I couldn't verbalize. I didn't know if anyone would read it, so it became a place of truth-telling, a way for me to process my thoughts honestly and without fear. And yet it became so much more than that.

Over time other parents of children with disabilities

found me and started leaving comments. They shared their own stories and struggles. This flowed over from my Facebook page and a community formed. It was through this community that God used special people in mighty ways who changed our lives forever.

But it never would have happened if I hadn't taken the first step and put myself out there.

The same is true with God. He works in mysterious ways and promises to provide for us, but He requires us to do our part too. It's hard for me to ask for things and even harder to accept help when it is offered. But if we refuse to be helped because of our pride, we block someone from being a blessing and being used by God.

In the Bible is a story of a widow with debts so enormous that her creditor was going to enslave her sons. She owned nothing except one jar of oil. It was at her most desperate hour that the prophet Elisha intervened. He instructed her to go ask her neighbors for as many jars and pots as she could find.

When she came back to the house, Elisha told her to pour the oil from her jar into all the remaining empty jars. She did so, and oil poured forth until all were filled. She was able to pay her debts, and she and her sons were able to live on the money from the rest of the oil that was left. (See 2 Kings 4.)

There is a difference between always having your hand out and asking for help when you really need it.

There are times when our needs are many and heavy, but there are other times when we can fill the jars of others.

I wonder how the widow felt going door to door borrowing jars and vessels from her neighbors. She may have been embarrassed to expose the severity of her situation to her community, but we know her neighbors helped her, for she had enough borrowed jars and pots to create an income to live on after paying her creditor.

God provides for us, but sometimes we have to step outside of our comfort zone. It was definitely out of my comfort zone to share with the world what was happening to our family. But because of that bravery and trust, we were able to receive fund-raising support and meet the amazing surgeon and specialists who continue to give Christian the best care possible.

God is an ever-present help, but He may require something of us. Let Him take you out of your comfort zone, whether that means asking others for help or being His hands and feet to meet someone else's need.

SEE GOD...

Is God asking you to step out of your comfort zone to help someone else or to ask help of others? If so, what has been stopping you? How has God used others to help you?

GIVE IT TO GOD IN PRAYER

Father, You are always good, whether I have plenty or little. I ask for the wisdom and humility to ask for help when You lead me to do so. When I have plenty, allow me to be a blessing to others, and when I have little, I choose to trust You to provide all my needs. In Jesus's name, amen.

Day 24

THE BLESSING OF FRIENDSHIP

Oil and perfume make the heart glad, and the sweetness of a friend comes from his earnest counsel.
—Proverbs 27:9, esv

GIRLFRIEND, WE NEED girlfriends. And guys… well, you need bro-time. Let's be honest.

We spend our days giving and pouring ourselves out to our family, jobs, and everyone around us. That's why it's so wonderful to have friends and loved ones who are willing to pour into us.

A special characteristic of my friends is that no matter how much time passes in between our visits or calls, it's as if no time has passed; it's like we saw each other yesterday. There's no pressure, no requirements that need to be met before my friends see me as "worth their time."

They graciously accept the busyness of our schedule.

Daily communication is nearly impossible, so they send texts when they think of me, and I do the same. When we are able to finally get together, we have tons of fun, picking up right where we left off.

A second attribute that my friends all seem to share is how well they pay attention and seem to pick up on *what* I need, *when* I need it. I don't usually have to ask them for help or a listening ear or a cup of coffee. Somehow they just seem to know. I pray that I can be so in tune to the needs of others that I can be half as perceptive and caring as my friends.

My friend Marisa is a perfect example. Her superpower is anticipating others' needs. When we stayed with her during Christian's surgeries, she literally thought of everything, from buying diapers for the kids to stocking her fridge with foods we love, including my favorite coffee creamer. She pays attention to the small things and quietly finds ways to lift our burden. Even the little details like the French Vanilla coffee creamer mean a whole lot.

When you find great friends, in person or online, treasure them. We live in a glorious age where we have the ability to stay in touch with one another instantly. When someone crosses your mind, send that person a text that says "Thinking of you" or "Hope you're doing well." If you find a thought-provoking article or hilarious meme, pass it on. These small gestures can keep a relationship going, especially when you live far away and can't talk every day.

Yet as fortunate as we are to have flesh-and-blood friends, we're even more fortunate that Jesus sees us, in part, as "friends." He said in John 15:15, "No longer do I call you servants, for the servant does not know what his master is doing; but I have called you friends, for all that I have heard from my Father I have made known to you" (ESV).

This doesn't mean that Jesus is our homeboy or our bestie. He is still God and worthy of the respect, awe, and wonder of His divinity. But the verse does show a shift in relationship after we choose to embrace Him as the One who died for our sins. While He is our Savior and King, He isn't distant or aloof.

Instead, as Bible teacher Charles Stanley so aptly observed, He accepts us, walks with us through trials, makes Himself available to us, and listens. These are the qualities of a good friend, and they are the attributes of our Lord.[1]

Even though we can't see Him, tweet Him, or hear His voice audibly, we can communicate with God anytime, anywhere. In fact, He will fill in the gaps when we don't know what to say. The Bible tells us, "In the same way the Spirit also helps our weakness; for we do not know how to pray as we should, but the Spirit

The Blessing of Friendship

Himself intercedes for us with groanings too deep for words" (Rom. 8:26, NASB).

That verse is deliciously chilling. We have God inside of us, and not only can we communicate with Him, but also He will even help facilitate that communication when we're overwhelmed or simply lost for words.

God has given me amazing friends, and I am so thankful I can draw comfort from their support when I'm sitting alone in a doctor's office waiting room or exhausted at home after a trying day. But even when I can't reach them, I am not alone. I have a Friend who understands my frailties, struggles, and hurts better than anyone (Heb. 2:18), and He helps me in those weak times by interceding before the Father when I don't know what to pray.

Friendship truly is sweet.

SEE GOD...

What are some ways Jesus has shown Himself to be not just your Savior but also your friend? What are some ways family and friends have supported you when you needed it?

_____

_____

Give It to God in Prayer

Father, thank You for being a Friend who will never leave me or forsake me. And thank You for the people You have placed in my life for me to share with, laugh with, and love with. Please bless each one richly. I ask for an abundance of blessings for each precious soul I have the privilege of calling "friend." In Jesus's name, amen.

Day 25

THE SMALL THINGS

*The LORD is my shepherd...he refreshes
my soul. He guides me along the
right paths for his name's sake.*
—PSALM 23:1, 3

WHEN GOD MOVES mountains, I can only fall on my face, overwhelmed by how magnificent He is. But sometimes it's the smaller blessings that have the deepest impact.

During our trip to Nationwide Children's Hospital (NCH) in Ohio, I knew God was doing something awesome. We were meeting with top specialists during complimentary consultations.

When we walked into NCH, I happened to glance at a brochure on the wall in the waiting room. Sticking out, in bright letters, was a pamphlet that read, "No surgery is routine when it's your child."

I stopped for a moment. My arms were laden with a diaper bag, purse, all my notes, and an extra jacket, all of which I almost dropped. I couldn't believe those words. It was like God said, "I know I've whispered this in your heart, but now I'm going to physically show you that your instincts are right on track."

I was overcome with God's goodness.

At this point in our journey several medical professionals had given me the impression that since all of Christian's surgeries were routine, I was "strange" for being worried.

What was I supposed to do? Be excited that my three-day-old son was undergoing surgery? Act nonchalant when my baby has an eight-hour operation at three months of age?

I truly believe this small pamphlet-gesture was from God. I don't know why my eyes were drawn to that brochure at that exact moment, but I knew God was telling me everything was going to be OK. I felt a rush of peace and thanked Him for the small reminder that He is in control and He is directing my path.

> The LORD is my shepherd.... He gives me new
> strength. He guides me in the right paths, as
> he has promised.
> —PSALM 23:1, 3, GNT

I love God's promises. I know the entire Bible is God-breathed truth, but when the Scripture specifically says He guides us in the right paths "as He

The Small Things

promised," I get a little giddy inside. God does guarantee us certain things, and He intends to keep those promises every time.

In Psalm 23:3 God not only promises to guide us on the right path but also to give us *new* strength. Heaven knows I need new strength. Do you have days when you're so exhausted and spent that you literally collapse on your bed? During those moments I think, "How will I ever get up and do this again tomorrow?"

We must cling to God's promises when things are difficult. His promises are fuel for my soul, reminders that God's plan for me is good (Jer. 29:11), that He will supply all my needs according to the riches of His glory (Phil. 4:19), and that He will always be with me, even to the end of days (Matt. 28:20).

Our God is great, and His mercies are new every morning (Lam. 3:22–23). The truth of the matter is that God knows exactly what we need, and He promises to give strength and guidance when we need it.

SEE GOD...

Describe some of the small moments when God showed up in your life. Describe some of the big moments. How did these moments build your faith?

_____

_____

Give It to God in Prayer

Father, I know You are for me. I will cling to Your promises when the road looks dark. Help me to see Your blessings, even the ones I've been taking for granted. Help me to become aware of Your goodness in the small things so I can truly appreciate Your majesty and goodness. In Jesus's name, amen.

Day 26

DEALING WITH SETBACKS

Behold, we consider those blessed who remained steadfast. You have heard of the steadfastness of Job, and you have seen the purpose of the Lord, how the Lord is compassionate and merciful.
—JAMES 5:11, ESV

DO YOU KNOW what it's like to feel completely aligned with God's will? Your prayers are answered, and you're confident in your walk with the Lord. You sense that He is directing your path and that you're exactly where you're supposed to be. But then, just when you feel you're nearing your destination, you face a setback.

That's how I felt after a crucial visit with our son's plastic surgeon. We hadn't agreed with her when she diagnosed Christian with craniosynostosis, another extremely rare birth defect that would require a deeply invasive and extremely dangerous operation on his skull. Chris and I did our due diligence and sought second and third opinions from other experts. Yet after having more than one team of specialists say Christian did *not* have this second disorder, our surgeon still refused to agree.

I felt like all the work we'd done was for nothing, and we were now going backward.

Some days it seemed like no matter how much we did, no matter how hard we worked, we just couldn't get ahead. Developmentally Christian was months behind his peers in terms of hitting the milestones set for him, no matter how many hours we invested in therapies and practice. It was frustrating because other children didn't need hours of therapy every week, plus extra hours of work at home to hit their milestones.

At times it was painful to watch Christian struggle to do things that came naturally to other kids, but eventually God taught me to stop comparing Christian. It did us no good to focus on the obstacles. I had to celebrate the triumphs, no matter how small.

When I learned to shift my focus from the setbacks to the successes, my attitude and perspective totally changed. I no longer moped because Christian was struggling. Instead, I was thrilled each time he gained a new skill or accomplished a goal, no matter how minor. My weeping turned into joy.

Dealing With Setbacks

Setbacks happen. We can lay out our plans, review the contingencies, and pray for the best. But still things will go wrong. A child will have to go potty just as you are leaving the house. Someone will throw up. The keys that are always on the hook by the door will mysteriously vanish. The car that you filled with gas yesterday will be sitting on empty when you're in a hurry.

I've come to "expect the unexpected." Yet sometimes the "unexpected-unexpected" happens.

Scripture has so many stories of people who dealt with obstacles. The Israelites were delivered from slavery in Egypt only to find themselves hungry in the wilderness. Nehemiah's task was to build a wall, but the process was interrupted time and again. Job was known as a prosperous man, rich both personally and professionally, but in a mind-bogglingly short time span he lost his children and his livelihood. Poor guy.

When they faced a setback, the Israelites grumbled. It's as if they forgot that God literally parted a sea so they could escape their captors. They had physically seen God miraculously lead them out of Pharaoh's grip and away from persecution, but still their faith had limits.

Because of their complaints, their setback lasted longer than it had to. They wandered the wilderness for forty years, until the faithless generation had died out.

Job and Nehemiah, on the other hand, had a different testimony. Although Job endured more heartache and loss than most of us could possibly imagine, he didn't deny God. His faith remained steadfast, and God blessed him beyond measure, restoring his wealth and giving him more children to keep his legacy alive.

And because Nehemiah knew God had given him a directive—that rebuilding the wall around Jerusalem wasn't just his own idea—he remained at the wall. He saw its construction through to completion even when other pressing matters sought to pull him away.

When we face setbacks, we have a choice to make. We can be like the Israelites and lose faith, grumbling and complaining and acting as if God has done nothing for us in the past. Or we can follow the example of Nehemiah and Job. We can remember all the things God has done and choose to continue to trust Him, knowing that He doesn't lead us to leave us.

SEE GOD...

Think back over the past few days or weeks. What setbacks have popped up in your life? How did you deal with those unexpected situations? What can you do in the future to remain steadfast in faith when setbacks come?

_____

_____

Dealing With Setbacks

GIVE IT TO GOD IN PRAYER

Dear God, I know setbacks are going to come my way, but when they do, help me to remember Your goodness so I don't lose faith. Let me sense Your presence and know You will be beside me the whole time. Hold me in Your hand. Protect me and keep me safe. And when the way is clear please set my feet on solid ground. Father, I trust You, for You are good. In Jesus's name, amen.

Day 27

THE GIFT OF NO

*And this same God who takes care of me [Paul]
will supply all your needs from his glorious riches,
which have been given to us in Christ Jesus.*
—Philippians 4:19, NLT

When God says no to our earthly wants and desires, it's because He has other plans in mind. Sometimes a no is really a "not now," and sometimes a no is God's way of protecting us.

For nineteen months I fought with our insurance company to let Christian receive care outside of Tennessee. We were in a no-win situation. The only specialist who would perform the critical cleft palate operation was the surgeon who diagnosed Christian with craniosynostosis and wanted to cut through his skull. Other specialists disagreed, and yet this doctor wouldn't budge on the diagnosis. And now no other insurance-covered specialist would take our case.

I found the hospital of my dreams, but it was out of

The Gift of No

network and out of state. I exhausted every possible avenue I could think of with our insurance company, including taking them to court.

Verdict: motion denied.

For nineteen months I was scared and uncertain about what would happen or when it would happen, but I could not deny that God was in the midst of the anguish, busily connecting the dots and laying everything in place. Instead of constant battles, circumstances began to fall into place, with little or no effort on my end. As I watched in amazement as events unfolded, it was clear that God had let me fight, and He was now showing me His greatness, goodness, and mercy. It was time to rest in Him.

When I received an offer from a stranger for us to receive a consultation at a prestigious children's hospital in another state, I knew God was moving. Through that experience we met the *right* surgeon, the man who did more for Christian's care than I ever would have thought possible.

Looking back, I see how God's no led to a better yes. If our insurance company had acquiesced to the first hospital, we may never have connected with the surgeon who became our hero. He intervened for us with the insurance company, and they decided to cover the surgery at this new hospital.

God knew what He was doing, even if it took nineteen months for me to finally understand.

The prophet Jeremiah could probably relate. I imagine, like most other men in his community, Jeremiah would have liked to get married and start a family. Yet God told him, "You shall not take a wife, nor shall you have sons or daughters in this place" (Jer. 16:2, MEV).

I feel a little sorry for him. He was to spend a lifetime in service to God without the support of a family.

If you've ever been in ministry or are close to someone who is, you know the stress it can bring. It's crucial to have a support system, but here we see that God told Jeremiah not to marry and have children.

We don't serve a heavenly Father who is cruel. He explains in Jeremiah 16 why it was in Jeremiah's best interest to stay single.

> For this is what the LORD says about the sons and daughters born in this land and about the women who are their mothers and the men who are their fathers: "They will die of deadly diseases. They will not be mourned or buried but will be like dung lying on the ground. They will perish by sword and famine, and their dead bodies will become food for the birds and the wild animals."
>
> —JEREMIAH 16:3–4

The Gift of No

When we see the picture from God's perspective, it's possible to think God's no was a gift. Perhaps God was sparing Jeremiah the agony and heartbreak of loss. As a parent who wishes any and all pain could be transferred from my children to me, I think this is significant, even though it had to be difficult for Jeremiah to be alone.

God doesn't always tell us why He says no to our requests, and I don't know if understanding why God told him not to marry brought Jeremiah any comfort. But I do know this: when God tells us no, it's because He has a reason, and that reason usually means He has an even better yes for us on the horizon.

SEE GOD...

How many times has God told you no? How do you determine that His answer is no instead of "not now"? How do you react to the disappointment?

_____

_____

_____

_____

_____

Give It to God in Prayer

Father, You're going to tell me yes, and You're going to tell me no. Please help me to be patient and know that despite my disappointment, You have all things under control and will meet my needs. In Jesus's name, amen.

Day 28

STICKS AND STONES

*The heart of the righteous ponders how to answer,
but the mouth of the wicked pours out evil things.*
—Proverbs 15:28, ESV

WORDS STING.

After I started blogging, I was exposed to the best and the worst social media have to offer. I met people online who encouraged me and became true friends, people whose love and kindness were a lifeline during our early years with Christian. But the Internet also exposed us to the darkness in people's hearts.

People will say things on social media that they would never say to your face. Along with name-calling and negativity, Chris and I were even accused of Photoshop-editing Christian's face to get sympathy and using his disability to selfishly raise money for ourselves.

Nastiness is expected in certain social circles. The

movie *Mean Girls* portrays this perfectly. It could be said that it's a win for our culture that we're willing to admit that there are mean girls (and guys) in the world. But knowing that meanness is common doesn't make it any easier to deal with.

Too often criticism and condemnation from heartless strangers can make us pause for just a second too long, wondering if there is any validity to the person's claim. Even people who don't know you can wound you with their words.

Yet even when the worst things in the world are spoken, God calls us to love. We must remember that the words of cruel strangers do not, in any way, define us. We are who God says we are: Loved. Righteous. His.

Words hurt, but God is the healer of broken hearts. Whenever someone says something nasty about Christian, it stings because he is my son and I love him. But it doesn't leave a wound because I know that what they've said is not true. Those words are false.

I *know* Christian. He isn't a monster. He is fearfully and wonderfully made because God said so. And God says the same thing about the rest of us. People can talk, and they will, but the fact that ugly words spew from their lips doesn't make them true. And when the words hurt, we have to remember that God cares for us and will heal our hearts despite what people say.

We have to pay attention to whom we are listening

to. Are we letting God tell us who we are, or are we letting the world tell us?

If you've ever experienced cruelty, you know how devastating the results can be. Words linger and haunt us in our minds. But our true character is often revealed in how we react. Sometimes we "Christianize" our lack of self-respect by excusing the cruel behavior and "turning the other cheek." I think there are times when we need to not worry about appearing like a crazed mama bear and stand our ground.

It is truth that empowers, truth that heals, truth that sets free. When the mean girls (or guys) start spewing their hateful words, remind yourself of what is true. And if God calls you to confront the haters, speak the truth, but do it in love.

SEE GOD...

Describe a situation in which you were able to respond to someone in love instead of reacting with anger. Are there words that have been said to you that you can't let go of? If so, how do those words compare with who God says you are?

_____

_____

Give It to God in Prayer

Father, help me to forget the cruel words that linger in my heart. Remind me of who You say I am. I thank You that I am Yours! In Jesus's name, amen.

Day 29

GOD THE RESTORER

And after you have suffered a little while, the God of all grace, who has called you to his eternal glory in Christ, will himself restore, confirm, strengthen, and establish you.
—1 Peter 5:10, esv

WHEN I THINK about restoration, I think of DIY projects, like turning a chest of drawers into a little girl's glitzed-out mini-wardrobe, or sanding down a fine piece of furniture and applying fresh protective lacquer or stain. It's about taking something that is slightly used and faded and making it beautiful again. Through restoration the piece looks better than the original.

Christian had so many extra needs when he was born that Chris and I were separated from him during the first few months of his life. He was in the NICU for a month, then at endless appointments, tests, therapies, and even in surgery. There were so many small experiences that we missed out on, and at times I mourned those losses.

God restored my aching heart by surprising me with Chandler, our second baby. I know this isn't always the way God restores a broken heart, but it wasn't until I experienced a "typical pregnancy" and was allowed to deliver Chandler naturally, hold him immediately after he was born, and enjoy all the new baby experiences I'd only heard other moms talk about that I realized God had given me a precious gift.

God restored my early days of motherhood.

He restored my heart.

First Peter 5:10 says, "And the God of all grace, who called you to his eternal glory in Christ, after you have suffered a little while, will himself restore you and make you strong, firm steadfast." I know the term *suffering* in this verse has to do with being persecuted for following Jesus. But when I read this verse recently, it touched my heart in a deep way and opened my eyes to God's heart for us when we go through other types of suffering.

We will all experience suffering. Living as a Christian isn't easy. Life isn't easy for nonbelievers either, but some people think following Jesus ensures they'll live a posh life, and that's just not true. This verse in 1 Peter 5 tells the real and honest truth. As a follower of Christ you will suffer, but after you've endured, God will restore.

God the Restorer

He fixes circumstances.

He fixes us.

Not only does God restore us, but the verse says He also confirms, strengthens, and establishes us. Those words mean He makes us stable, settles us on a firm foundation, and gives us strength. I love that.

But in order to be restored, we have to be willing to go through the process. Metal has to be heated to molten temperatures to be pliable enough to work with. And an old or antique piece of furniture may have to be scoured or scraped to remove old paint or damage and bring out the beauty underneath. Similarly we may have to let God turn up the heat in our lives or pull out His scouring pad to get rid of the hardness that has built up in our hearts. But restoration is worth it.

I want to be better than my original. The original Lacey is a sinner who expected God to fix all her problems and got angry when He didn't answer her prayers the way she thought He should. The restored Lacey knows that when heartache and despair push their way into her life, she can call out to Jesus, who will hold her in the midst of the storm.

See God...

What moments in your life has God restored? Are you in the restoration process currently? How has He been strengthening you through the process?

Give It to God in Prayer

Thank You, Father, for being a God of restoration and new beginnings! Thank You for not leaving me where I am but loving me enough to refine me. Though the process can be painful, let me ever praise You, for the painful times will make me healed and whole. In Jesus's name, amen.

Day 30

YOU ARE HIS MASTERPIECE

Yet you, LORD, are our Father. We are the clay, you are the potter; we are all the work of your hand.
—ISAIAH 64:8

THERE WAS A time early in Christian's life when a simple trip to the grocery store would take forever because of how often I would get stopped by people who were curious about his condition. It got to the point where I'd leave a lightweight blanket over his car seat so I could grab milk and bread and get home.

It was during one of these shopping trips that I heard God whisper, "Don't hide this baby."

That phrase stayed in my thoughts for a long time. Each time I'd drape the blanket over the car seat handle, I'd hear it echo in my heart. With each whisper I came to realize that Christian was indeed fearfully and wonderfully made, and that God had a much bigger plan for my son's life than I could ever have imagined.

God always provides us with what we need. If Christian had needed his eyesight to fulfill God's purpose for his life, then Christian would be able to see. We may feel like we lack special talents or skills, but God calls us, equips us, and creates a wonderful work in us despite what we perceive as flaws.

I believe God has an appreciation for beauty. Not only does He daily create magnificent sunrises and sunsets, but God also decorated His creation with beautiful splendor. Even the fish are beautifully clothed.

As a collective group humans also appreciate beauty. The Louvre in Paris had 8.6 million visitors in 2015 and over 9 million in 2014.[1] We are intrigued by the craftsmanship and talent of the artists. For some people this curiosity resides so deep that they choose to spend their lives dedicated to researching and analyzing the pieces.

Get this—according to a French scientist, the famous *Mona Lisa* painting is, in fact, hiding a second painting underneath.[2] Using special technology, both images can be compared side by side. It's fascinating to see how the mysterious *Mona Lisa* was transformed from the original. It's as if da Vinci said, "It's good, but I'm not finished revealing who you are."

I think God does that with us. He loves us where

You Are His Masterpiece

we are, but He wants to continually mold and shape us into an even more beautiful instrument for His glory.

I am a work of art, still in progress. So are you.

We are not mistakes.

We were created in God's image. He is the master potter and we are the clay—His beautiful creations with our own unique qualities. The trouble happens when we forget our roles and believe that we shape our future instead of God.

I stopped hiding Christian when I realized that he is God's masterpiece. Society can't always handle our differences. We can be made to feel like outcasts for having birth defects, disabilities, speech impediments, learning or behavior issues—the list goes on. We can be made to feel like we're worthless if we don't fit a certain mold. But that is the furthest thing from the truth.

God made each of us a masterpiece, and He can use even our weaknesses in ways we'd never imagine.

SEE GOD...

What areas of your life are you the most self-conscious about? How have you seen God turn your insecurities into confidence?

_____

_____

Give It to God in Prayer

Dear God, I want to be a world-changer. I want to do great things in Your name, but sometimes I feel insignificant or like I'm not qualified. Help me to remember that You made me and You qualify and equip me to do Your will. In Jesus's name, amen.

Day 31

THE POWER OF COMMUNITY

*Now you are the body of Christ, and
each one of you is a part of it.*
—1 Corinthians 12:27

It's hard to describe isolation. I was constantly surrounded by people who cared immensely about my family, about Christian, about everything that was going on. Yet somehow I still felt alone.

No one else really understood what I was going through. They did their best to be there for me and to try to meet our needs, but the one thing I really needed was someone who could say, "It's going to be OK. I made it through this, and you can too."

None of my friends or family could say that. This was new to all of us. They didn't know any more than I did how we were going to make it through.

When Christian was still in the NICU, my sweet mom saw how lonely I was, so she coordinated people to ride with me to Nashville each day to visit Christian. She didn't like that I was by myself all day, driving for hours alone. I'm so appreciative for the wonderful people who rode with me back and forth and sat with me as I walked through those early months like a zombie.

While the company was a wonderful gesture, I always felt like I had to be "on" when I was around people, especially if we weren't really close friends. My stress level was so high that I'd forget to even ask if my guest wanted lunch. I was barely remembering to eat as it was. I hope everyone who spent time with me during those early weeks understands how much I appreciate their kindness.

So, in a way, I desperately wanted to be alone, and yet I also desperately wanted someone who'd walked this road before me.

God filled this need in an interesting way. Someone created a Facebook fan page for Christian, and by the time I found out about it, there were already thirty-five thousand people following it. I was surprised that anyone outside of my immediate friends and family would have any interest in what was happening in our lives.

At that point God had already laid on my heart strict instructions that I was not to hide Christian from the world. God was causing all these things to fall into place.

The Power of Community

I didn't have control of it; it was just happening. The Facebook page, the viral YouTube video, the thousands of messages, the *Through the Eyes of Hope* book, this devotional—I didn't do it. I just sat still, watched God take over, and marveled at what He did when I stopped protesting long enough to listen and let Him work.

God used all these things to show me that I wasn't alone. Not only did He give me one or two friends, but He also gave me—us—a growing community of more than three hundred thousand people and extremely close friends from different parts of the country and all over the world whom I would never have known otherwise.

Community is powerful. The feeling of togetherness and belonging is critical for our sense of self. It's also beneficial when we're going through a crisis. There's a reason twelve-step programs use meetings, why churches develop small groups, and why there are literally hundreds of millions of Facebook groups online.

We desire to connect with like-minded individuals, and when we're in crisis mode, this community becomes a lifeline.

As Christ-followers we are part of a huge community. We have thousands upon thousands of brothers and sisters around the world. And this community is eternal.

Each of us has a part to play in making the body of Christ a life-giving community. When we're not the ones going through a hard time, we need to be there for others. We have to encourage one another and be supportive. We have to be the hands and feet of Jesus.

God likened His followers to a body because we are meant to function together. He never intended for us to be independent and alone but rather interdependent on one another. Pastor Rick Warren noted that there is no deeper fellowship than the fellowship of suffering, where we enter one another's pain.[1]

I'm so grateful for the people who stepped up and brought meals, watched Christian for a couple of hours so I could get to law school on time, and just stopped by to check on us and cuddle my sweet baby. This is how we demonstrate the power of community, when we choose to bear one another's burdens and fellowship with those who are suffering. Oftentimes it's the small things, an extra step of service, that make all the difference.

SEE GOD...

How has God brought people into your life to be your community? How can you serve someone in your community?

_____

_____

GIVE IT TO GOD IN PRAYER

Father, thank You for the support system that You have put in place in my life. I pray that You would strengthen and encourage them when they are down, and I pray that they would continually look to You for strength. Please bless those who have been Your hands and feet in my life; lift them up and remind them that You are with them wherever they go. Give me discernment to know whom You have placed in my life and those You haven't. In Jesus's name, amen.

Day 32

WILLING TO LEARN

The heart of the discerning acquires knowledge, for the ears of the wise seek it out.
—Proverbs 18:15

There is a steep learning curve when it comes to raising a child with a disability. I researched every piece of information I could find about Tessier clefts, and I know that parents in similar situations did the same thing with their children's conditions.

Sometimes I think parents know more about the disability or condition their children have been diagnosed with than anyone. It's not just the fact that they spend an exorbitant amount time researching the diagnosis, but also because they deal with the disability every hour of every day. We see that same type of dedication in students prepping for the SAT, spelling bee contestants, Olympic hopefuls, job interviewers—the list goes on and on.

When we love something or someone, it's amazing

Willing to Learn

what lengths we will go to. Our dedication may even border on obsession, but it's because we want to learn.

The Special Kids Therapy & Nursing Center is an organization designed to help children with special needs. Their mission is to serve Jesus by caring for His children,[1] and they became my lifeline.

The therapists taught Christian to walk by first teaching him to stand at a toy for longer and longer periods of time to build muscle strength. When he was ready, they then taught him to shift his weight by moving from one foot to the other. Then they moved to taking steps, one at first, then two, and so on.

This was a *sloooow* process, and on its own each tiny piece of the puzzle seemed small and insignificant. But these trained professionals knew that every piece had to be in its place for the end goal to be reached. And so finally Christian took his first steps at twenty-seven months of age. It was a miraculous day.

Beyond helping Christian achieve important milestones, the Special Kids Community was invaluable to us. They taught me without realizing it as I watched how they interacted with Christian and the different methods they used to achieve milestone goals. If we want to learn, we have to choose people to learn from, and we have to choose them wisely.

> The heart of the prudent gets knowledge, and
> the ear of the wise seeks knowledge.
> —Proverbs 18:15, MEV

When God told King Solomon that he could ask for anything he wanted, Solomon asked for wisdom and knowledge. It could be said that Solomon showed an inkling of wisdom before he asked for it, since Proverbs 18:15 says that the "ears of the wise seek out" knowledge.

What's interesting about Solomon is that he wasn't kneeling beside his bed one night, saying his sleepy time prayers when he asked God for wisdom. And God didn't speak to Solomon out of the blue.

It was after Solomon spent time working (public speaking is no joke, you know!) and worshipping (by presenting a sacrifice) that God offered to give Solomon whatever he asked. (See 2 Chronicles 1:6.) The kid in me thinks about the movie *Aladdin* and the genie's three wishes. Shouldn't Solomon have asked for infinite requests? Did he blow it? #JustKidding.

Solomon made the right choice. He asked for the wisdom he needed to complete the assignment God had given him: to lead his nation.

While you and I may never have that level of responsibility on our shoulders, God wants us to seek His wisdom to complete the assignments He has given us. I ask for wisdom to serve my family, to respect my husband, to lead my children. For me it's the most precious responsibility in the world and one I'm willing to learn.

God may not offer to give us anything we want as He did with Solomon, but the God who "gives generously to all without finding fault" has promised to give us wisdom (James 1:5). All we have to do is ask for it.

SEE GOD...

Have you ever asked God specifically for wisdom and knowledge? If not, why not ask Him now? How has God shown you that He has blessed you with those attributes?

_____

_____

_____

_____

GIVE IT TO GOD IN PRAYER

Dear God, I ask for wisdom and knowledge, the gift you gave to King Solomon. Help me to be wise in how I manage my household, my finances, my relationships, and even everyday situations. In Jesus's name, amen.

Day 33

GOD LOOKS AT THE HEART

The LORD does not look at the things people look at. People look at the outward appearance, but the LORD looks at the heart.
—1 SAMUEL 16:7

As the mother of a child with a facial disability, I find that I have a high sensitivity to anything related to appearance—quotes, memes, jokes, even Bible verses. I was reading through 1 Samuel and the popular verse hit me—"People look at the outward appearance, but the LORD looks at the heart."

Jesus wasn't a physically attractive man. Even though He would probably have had super strong muscles since He was a stonemason by trade (yup, that's a better translation of *carpenter*), the Bible says in Isaiah 53:2 that Jesus had "no beauty or majesty to attract us." It was His personality, His charisma, His message of

God Looks at the Heart

truth that drew people to Him. People saw God in Him. He was, after all, God in the flesh.

When I look at my sweet baby boy, his face still healing from his surgeries, I don't see the pink tissue where his eyes didn't form. I don't notice the scars running down the side of his face to his lips. All I see is the spirited little guy who loves to play the piano and push his brother off the bed.

I see a little boy who loves to giggle and wants to be independent.

I see my son's heart.

When God told the prophet Samuel that "it's what is on the inside that counts," he was in the process of anointing a new king of Israel. Samuel had gone to the home of Jesse, knowing one of his sons would be the next king, and when he saw Jesse's son Eliab, he thought he had surely found Israel's new ruler. Eliab looked like royalty. But God reminded Samuel that what we see on the outside isn't what's important.

The Lord looks at our heart.

Society places a premium on our appearance, and for good reason. Our appearance is our first impression. We "judge a book by the cover" and "eat with our eyes." But beauty is in the eye of the beholder. And the Bible says it is fleeting (Prov. 31:30).

King David was undesirable before he was crowned. He was not only the youngest brother in a long line of sons (strike one), but also his job as shepherd was the worst of the worst (strike two). But unlike Saul, David was "a man after [God's] own heart" (1 Sam. 13:14). And that made all the difference. David became Israel's greatest king and was part of the lineage of Jesus.

When we die, we leave behind but the shell of who we are. Our hearts are what God sees and what will last. There's nothing wrong with taking care of our outward appearance so long as it doesn't come at the expense of our internal beauty. To God, the kind of person we are is what's important. He wants us to radiate the fruit of His Spirit—love, joy, peace, patience, kindness, goodness, faithfulness, gentleness, and self-control (Gal. 5:22–23). Cultivating these positive attributes is truly the best beauty secret around.

SEE GOD...

Are you a person after God's heart, as David was? Will you do everything He wants you to do? If not, what is stopping you?

_____

_____

_____

GIVE IT TO GOD IN PRAYER

Father, help me to develop the qualities You see as valuable rather than what the world values. Give me eyes to see others the way you see them, not by what they look like on the outside, but by their heart. Give me eyes to see myself through Your eyes too, Lord. When I fall into that trap of playing the comparison game, remind me that You have created me and called me according to Your purpose, and those things, not my appearance, are what truly matter. Father, Your works are wonderful, I know that full well! In Jesus's name, amen.

Day 34

AT WORK BEHIND THE SCENES

When you pass through the waters, I will be with you; and through the rivers, they shall not overwhelm you; when you walk through fire you shall not be burned, and the flame shall not consume you.
—Isaiah 43:2, ESV

During every one of Christian's surgeries I struggle with handing my baby over to a surgical team and being separated from him for hours. I worry over how he must be feeling, and I hate knowing that he will soon wake up in pain, confused and scared.

I struggle with not knowing the outcome of the surgery until it's over. I even struggle with God, wondering if He'll answer my prayers in the way I hope. What I wouldn't give to know the outcome of the surgery beforehand. Then I'd know exactly what to do: "No, we won't have this surgery," or "Yes, go ahead!"

But God doesn't give me that foresight, so I simply have to trust Him during those times when I can't see what lies ahead. I have to follow Scripture and walk by faith and not by sight (2 Cor. 5:7).

> When you pass through the waters, I will be with you. And through the rivers, they shall not overflow you. When you walk through fire, you shall not be burned, nor shall the flame kindle on you.
>
> —Isaiah 43:2, mev

Our heavenly Father knows what the future holds; He sees the map of our life—the elusive mountains, the scary valleys, the sunny hilltops of happiness. And He is with us through the journey.

That gives me a lot of comfort. I'm not alone when I'm sitting helpless in the surgical waiting area. I'm not alone when I'm drowning under a sea of insurance paperwork. None of us are ever alone, even when we feel the loneliest.

We will have problems in this life. The Bible doesn't deny it. In fact, Jesus said in John 16:33 that we will have tribulation. Isaiah 43:2 says *"when* you walk through the fire," letting us know that we will walk through flames in life. Yet God promises that we won't be consumed or burned.

Walking through fire doesn't sound that great. Neither does passing through waters that will overwhelm me. Yet I can look back at the hard times in my life and I know—I *know*—that God walked me through each one. I may feel alone and helpless, but He's with me. He's even living inside of me as the Great Comforter, my ever-present help in time of trouble.

While it's scary to think about the hard times that will come—and probably have already come—we can trust that God is working behind the scenes. He will take care of us and provide for us.

SEE GOD...

What mountaintop or valley are you living in right now? How has God shown you that He is with you in the deep waters of life?

_____

_____

_____

_____

_____

Give It to God in Prayer

Father, help me trust You when I can't see the road ahead. I may not be able to see past the twists and turns, but You're holding the directions. Thank You for being the God who leads us. In Jesus's name, amen.

Day 35

MODERN-DAY MIRACLES

*Behold, these are but the outskirts of his ways,
and how small a whisper do we hear of him! But
the thunder of his power who can understand?*
—JOB 26:14, ESV

SOME PEOPLE HAVE a hard time believing in miracles, but God absolutely shows up in inexplicable ways.

The procedure to surgically close Christian's palate was especially challenging. A "hard to close" palate typically ranges from 10mm to 12mm wide. Christian had an 18mm-wide cleft, and our plastic surgeon didn't think the tissue from each side would reach. The plan was to fill in the gap with tissue from Christian's throat.

From. His. Throat.

This was a dangerous surgery, a brand-new procedure created specifically for Christian that had never been done before. The skin from the back of Christian's throat had to be pulled forward. If it swelled, it would block his airway. We had been praying specifically for that part of the procedure to go well.

God answered in bigger ways than we expected.

We were praying fervently, and we asked those who had been following us on social media, our church family, our friends, and our loved ones to be praying for us as well.

I stayed up late and prayed. And cried.

Before Christian's surgery his doctor met us in one of the patient rooms. Chris and I sat in the rigid chairs while Christian lay tight against me, clutching my arms.

Chris spoke first. "We think the palate closed a little."

"It honestly looks smaller," I confirmed.

The doctor looked from Chris to me, down at Christian, and then back to Chris. Every millimeter counted. He furrowed his brow momentarily, but ever the professional, he nodded at us. "That just doesn't happen," he said, "but I'll measure to be safe."

Chris carried Christian to the pre-operating area. We kissed him and whispered prayers in his ears until a nurse came to get him.

And God showed up.

A few hours later Christian's doctor pushed through the double doors of the surgical area and strode over to us in the waiting room. Everyone moved as close as they could without imposing.

"You'll never believe it," he said, "but the palate *was* narrower than the last surgery. We didn't have to cut the tissue from his throat." The joy on his face was unmistakable. He'd been able to close the hole just as he would any other cleft palate.

There was no medical explanation for how Christian's palate narrowed; it was a miraculous grace that protected Christian from a dangerous new procedure. And we give God all the glory.

While we truly believe God performed a miracle of healing in Christian's body, I know what it's like to wonder why my baby couldn't be miraculously and completely healed. We don't know why God chooses to answer certain prayers in the affirmative. Why does He heal certain people and let others remain in pain? I don't have the answers, and I'm not sure it would help if we knew why.

This is what I am sure of: God is good even when He says no.

There are countless stories of people who had advanced-stage cancer only to go to the doctor's office one day and be told that no cancer cells could be found. And there are those with testimonies of God healing emotional wounds and mending broken hearts.

I have asked God for small things so many times. The

requests were so insignificant I almost feel guilty for wasting His time. But I ask anyway, because it's a lie that God doesn't care about what we care about. He absolutely does. So I bring the big and small prayers, concerns, and desires of my heart to the One who calls me *child*.

I don't always get my way. I don't always see healing, but I do believe beyond the shadow of a doubt that God did something miraculous for my son in the hospital that day. He closed Christian's palate within a millimeter of what was needed for the operation to be a success. It was a minute difference, but the ramifications were huge.

"Indeed, these are but a part of His ways, and how small a whisper we hear of Him! But the thunder of His power who can understand?" (Job 26:14, MEV*).*

With Christian's cleft closing by the tiniest millimeter before his surgery, we saw the amazing power of God.

Proven power.

Soft murmurs.

Whispers.

God answers our prayers in His way and in His timing. But we must never forget that He is powerful, and He still works miracles on our behalf.

See God...

Has God ever performed a miracle in your life or the life of someone close to you? How did the experience build your faith?

_____

_____

_____

_____

_____

_____

Give It to God in Prayer

Lord, I trust Your goodness. When storms come and oceans rage, may I remain steadfast, knowing that You still perform miracles, and that no matter how You answer my prayers, it will be well with my soul. I give you all the praise. In Jesus's name, amen.

Day 36

STEP OUT

The LORD will fulfill his purpose for me; your steadfast love, O Lord, endures forever. Do not forsake the work of your hands.
—PSALM 138:8, ESV

I LOVE BEING ABLE to share Christian's and our story of faith with the world and thereby share Jesus with the world. It's a responsibility that I treasure, but having this new God-given platform makes me feel...strange.

In one sense I don't feel like I deserve such an amazing opportunity as this, to be able to share my heart with thousands upon thousands of people on a daily basis. I also feel humbled that God would use me and Christian in such a powerful way to spread the good news of Jesus.

It's also exciting that I get to do this—speak to people through books and public engagements. Having this opportunity is exhilarating, exhausting in a good way, and inspiring to me. It's been an honor to be interviewed on national media and speak before large crowds. Even though I never thought our lives would take this path, I wouldn't want to change it.

One of the most important lessons I've learned on this journey is that when God gives you a platform, you have a responsibility to do something with it. I've been pushed so far out of my comfort zone I barely even remember where it is. I feel like I'm on a ship so far from the shore, all I can see is water. But I want to use every opportunity I've been given to give God glory, which is why I choose to follow Him instead of holding on to what is familiar.

If I could give one piece of advice, it would be this: surrender to God's plan for you. Don't fight Him by telling Him what your gifts and abilities are and aren't. He already knows. Moses had a conversation like that with God. And guess what? Moses's fears and excuses didn't change God's mind. And that was a good thing—for Moses, for the people he was called to lead out of bondage, and for the people who needed to witness the power of God.

We should never want to win an argument with God.

In the Gospel of Luke, when Jesus called Peter, He told him, "Launch out into the deep and let down your nets for a catch" (Luke 5:4, MEV). After fishing all night, Peter had nothing to show for it. But because Jesus asked him to cast his nets in deeper water, he obliged.

And the nets filled to the point they could hardly contain the abundance.

With His instruction Jesus was inviting Peter to push himself further to reap a harvest he'd never experienced. And He invites us to do the same.

I cherish the opportunities God has given me to glorify His name, because I know God hasn't given everyone the same calling. Yet God is calling all of us to move beyond our comfort zone and reach out to others.

When we do, it creates a ripple effect. When I'm able to reach one person, who knows what God will do in that individual's heart? That person may reach more people than I will ever have the opportunity to touch. That's how the gospel spreads—one person, one opportunity at a time.

I believe God puts us exactly where He wants us to reach those around us. We just have to be willing to step out.

SEE GOD...

In what ways has God been calling you out of your comfort zone? Are you making excuses? Is something keeping you from surrendering to God?

_____

_____

Give It to God in Prayer

Father, help me to be brave enough to step out of my comfort zone and give You free rein to use me as You see fit. I want to go out into deep waters, to grow deeper in my faith and trust in You. Help me to surrender to You so I can accomplish Your will. In Jesus's name, amen.

Day 37

WORLD-CHANGERS

Therefore, take up the whole armor of God, that you may be able to withstand in the evil day, and having done all, to stand firm.
—Ephesians 6:13, ESV

If we want to see change happen, we have to be willing to *be* that change. Even when it isn't popular. Even when it's scary.

Sometimes we feel such a need to be accepted that we go with the status quo or do things we would never do just to fit in. Interestingly there was a YouTube video of a sociological experiment that proved just that.

The woman being observed walked into a doctor's office waiting room. The other people in the room had previously been instructed to stand up every time they heard a chime. This happened several times, but after the second or third time the woman stood as well.

Slowly the room emptied of everyone but the woman who had now been "trained" to stand when the chime was heard. Even when the waiting room was empty, she continued to stand. After a few minutes other people entered the waiting area who were unaware of the chimes. Slowly they all followed her lead and began to stand. The follower had become the leader, and none of them knew why they were standing.[1]

I hope I would have asked someone if I was in that situation.

If we can be so easily convinced to do things for no reason, think about the possibilities when someone is actually trying to persuade us. Peer pressure is a real thing, and if we're going to rise above following directions without question, we need to know what we believe and why we believe it.

We can't stand for no reason.

If we are going to be world-changers, we have to remain firm in God's truth. We have to face this world knowing that God has our back. I love the imagery in Ephesians 6, where we are instructed to put on the armor of God. You don't put something on by accident. Putting on the armor of God is a deliberate act, something we do to prepare for war, because every day we are in a battle to stand for truth in the midst of lies and deception.

The verse right before we're told to put on the armor of God says, "For our struggle is not against flesh and blood, but against the rulers, against the authorities, against the powers of this dark world and against the spiritual forces of evil in the heavenly realms" (Eph. 6:12).

I know God's Word is absolutely true, but to be honest, there were times I felt like I was fighting against flesh and blood. It was other humans who were vicious with their tongues and caused bitterness to fester in my heart.

The online bullies who made snide remarks about Christian's disability made me sensitive to the idea of fitting in. I wished Christian looked like other kids because I didn't want him to be teased about things he can't control. But in the midst of my wishing I learned an important lesson: fitting in is overrated.

People get so caught up with fitting in that they don't stop to think that maybe they're not supposed to.

If we take a look through history, it wasn't the average Joe who initiated significant change; it was the person who thought differently, acted differently. I want my children to follow Jesus, not the crowd. I want them to put on the armor of God so they can stand up in the face of evil, no matter in what form that torment presents itself.

We won't be world-changers if we constantly try to maintain the status quo. But our actions don't have to be grand either. It's the small things we do in the everyday, the purposeful decisions we make that end up changing our world.

SEE GOD...

Have you been in a situation where you had to stand up for your faith? How can you step out of your comfort zone, even in a small way, to become a world-changer?

___

___

___

___

GIVE IT TO GOD IN PRAYER

Father, it's hard to ignore the beckoning of society to fit in and follow the crowd, but You didn't call me to that. You have called me to follow You. You have called me to not be conformed to this world. Help me to overcome that temptation and instead to listen to Your voice and who You have called me to be. Remind me of Your calling on my life when I am struggling with peer pressure. In Jesus's name, amen.

Day 38

THE MYTH OF CONTROL

He got up, rebuked the wind and said to the waves, "Quiet! Be still!" Then the wind died down and it was completely calm. He said to his disciples, "Why are you so afraid? Do you still have no faith?"
—Mark 4:39–40

When you spin a top across a hard surface, the top rotates in a perfect circle, at least for a little while. As it begins to slow down, the top begins to wobble and the arc's rotation gets wider and wider until the top stops moving and falls on its side.

Kaput.

When life got that way, I didn't have my focus on God but instead on all the things I needed to "control." Sometimes I forget that God is the only person I can trust enough to actually relax. His attributes are love and kindness. His plans are good.

Honestly I never had control. It was an illusion. God knows what we need, and it doesn't always add up to what we want. The more I struggled with trying to control everything, from finances to the schedule, the more I felt like I was spinning out of control.

Submission to God is not about having Him control you, but rather it's about falling in love with the Creator of the universe and trusting Him with your life, the life He created.

There is comfort in knowing someone has your back. The hard part comes when we don't know exactly what is coming.

The disciples learned this truth in the midst of a terrifying storm.

> That day when evening came, [Jesus] said to his disciples, "Let us go over to the other side." Leaving the crowd behind, they took him along, just as he was, in the boat. There were also other boats with him. A furious squall came up, and the waves broke over the boat, so that it was nearly swamped. Jesus was in the stern, sleeping on a cushion. The disciples woke him and said to him, "Teacher, don't you care if we drown?"

The Myth of Control

> He got up, rebuked the wind and said to the waves, "Quiet! Be still!" Then the wind died down and it was completely calm.
>
> He said to his disciples, "Why are you so afraid? Do you still have no faith?"
>
> They were terrified and asked each other, "Who is this? Even the wind and the waves obey him!"
>
> —Mark 4:35–41

The myth of control is that we think we have it. Ha! It's like the age-old saying, "If you want to hear God laugh, tell Him your plans." Sometimes God lays a dream in our heart and we feel like we're "controlling our destiny" when all we're doing is walking the journey He set before us.

It's just an illusion when we think we have control. We aren't in control of anything.

When the storms rose over the sea and the disciples were frightened, Jesus didn't even blink. Now, if you've ever been through a hurricane or tornado, you know how scary they can be. To have absolute dominion over a storm is amazing.

Jesus told the winds to be still, and they did. They had no choice but to obey the Creator of the universe. That's control.

When Job was upset, God asked if Job had set the stars in the sky or told the ocean how far it could come on the shore. I have a hard enough time getting my kids to listen to me, and yet the elements are in complete submission to God. It's crazy to think about when you try to wrap your mind around it.

The next time you feel like you're in control, try ordering the sun to stop shining. That will give you a little reality check. But the good news is that when we submit to the One who really is in control, He works everything together for our good and brings us through every storm.

SEE GOD...

When is the last time you thought you were in control of a situation? Have you ever felt like you were in control only to have something backfire? How do you let God have control of your life?

_____

_____

_____

_____

_____

_____

GIVE IT TO GOD IN PRAYER

Dear God, I am not in control and I know it, but sometimes in the middle of a situation I act like I am. I forget that I serve the One who controls the wind and the waves. Help me to remember that no matter what is happening, I need to trust You because I can't make it through this life on my own. In Jesus's name, amen.

Day 39

CHOOSING FORGIVENESS

For if you forgive other people when they sin against you, your heavenly Father will also forgive you. But if you do not forgive others their sins, your Father will not forgive your sins.
—Matthew 6:14–15

When Christian was born, Chris and I dealt with the stress of our situation in completely opposite ways. I turned into a mama bear warrior, ever vigilant, ready to attack at the first sign of danger. Chris pulled away, immersing himself in work so he didn't have to think about the grief that was eating away at him. Because of this our relationship suffered immensely.

He saw me as too obsessed with Christian's care to take any time for anything else, including him. I saw Chris as uncaring, because I couldn't understand why he was not responding to the situation the same way I was. The truth is, neither of our reactions was necessarily right.

Everyone deals with grief and pain differently. That's what Chris and I did, and because we didn't communicate well, it caused a lot of hurt feelings. In all honesty, we both probably could have handled things differently and saved ourselves a lot of heartache, but hindsight is 20/20, as the saying goes.

At one point I knew our marriage was over.

Neither of us said it, but I knew.

I was angry. I felt betrayed. Through my hurt I saw no way that our marriage was salvageable. I had an opinion of what he should have been doing, and he wasn't doing it. Even if I had been right, I eventually had to realize that being right was not as important as being who God wants me to be.

Forgiveness is hard because it goes against everything you feel and think in those moments of pain. When we are hurt, we tend to feel anger and resentment toward the people who hurt us. We either want to stay far away from them or cause them pain in the way they have caused us to hurt. Nothing about our feelings says to be kind, but the thing about forgiveness is that forgiveness isn't for the person who hurt you. It's for you.

God calls us to a holy life, and holding on to resentment toward another person (a person whom He created and loves, by the way) does nothing for our holiness or our happiness.

It can take a long time to forgive someone. Sometimes it can take so long that you're "over it," yet hurt feelings remain below the surface, bubbling like an inferno when a memory is triggered. If the person who hurt you is someone you can't get away from, the scar from your wound gets picked like a scab.

There are times when you forgive and you know that you've let go and forgiven the person or people in your heart. But it can be hard to know you've forgiven when your feelings are hurt or you have been deeply wronged or betrayed. And sometimes you don't have a way to physically tell the person you forgive them, or it may be inappropriate to speak to them.

In the situations like these that are not cut and dry, how do you know if you've actually forgiven someone? I once heard someone say that when you have truly forgiven someone, you no longer seek to get even or punish the person. You give up the desire to see them "get what's coming to them," and you can sincerely pray that God forgives and blesses them.[1]

To put it simply, we wish them well. No wishing bad things upon them. Not being happy when something bad happens. No looking for them to be paid back for their behavior.

We forgive as Christ forgave us.

My marriage suffered until I let go of the weight of bitterness and resentment I felt toward Chris. It was a burden I shouldered, but I realized that until I forgave him, I wouldn't be free. I couldn't work on our marriage or have any sort of positive relationship with my husband until I let go.

This was not an easy process. It didn't happen overnight. It took years for us to get to the point we are now, and honestly we still have work to do.

Forgiveness doesn't mean we excuse the fact that someone did us wrong, because there are absolutely legitimate wrongs that are done to people. Forgiveness doesn't always mean we reconcile with someone either, though sometimes it does. Forgiveness can look different for every person and every situation, but whatever it looks like, forgiveness is God's will for us. As Christ forgave us, we must forgive others.

I promise, no matter how long it takes, forgiveness is worth it.

SEE GOD...

Is there someone in your life that you're harboring any anger or ill-will toward? If so, what is causing you to hold on to unforgiveness?

_____

_____

Give It to God in Prayer

Father, when I'm tempted to hold grudges, help me release the frustration, anger, and hurt so it doesn't turn to bitterness. Search my heart, and show me how I can forgive. Help me to easily release others in the future and wish them well. In Jesus's name, amen.

Day 40

REDEMPTION

*I will repay you for the years
the locusts have eaten.*
—Joel 2:25

In the Book of Genesis we meet a young man named Joseph who may understand betrayal better than anyone. Admittedly he was the spoiled baby of the family, the favored son. Yet Joseph's cushy life was drastically interrupted when his fed-up brothers threw him into a pit and sold him into slavery. Joseph's life was a whirlwind of labor and false accusations before he ended up in prison for several years.

I can't even imagine how discouraged and hopeless Joseph must have felt.

Fortunately things started to turn around. Pharaoh had a disturbing dream that he couldn't understand and that his trusted advisors couldn't explain. This is a beautiful demonstration of how God works out all things for good. See, Joseph had a God-given gift for interpreting people's dreams. In fact, it was Joseph's arrogance with this ability that festered hatred in his brothers' hearts so many years before.

After hearing the details of the dream, Joseph advised Pharaoh to store the harvests, aka Operation Save Egypt From Seven Years of Famine.

If you're familiar with this story, you know that Joseph became Pharaoh's right-hand man, a powerful and prestigious position. The famine he'd predicted caused his brothers to eventually come to Egypt seeking grain. After their reunion Joseph declared, "You intended to harm me, but God intended it for good to accomplish what is now being done, the saving of many lives" (Gen. 50:20).

God didn't cause all the bad things that happened to Joseph, but He knew all along how He was going to bring good out of them, how He would redeem them not only for Joseph's benefit but also for "the saving of many lives."

There's no doubt in my mind that Joseph thought his life was over as he rotted away, forgotten in his jail cell. I've certainly felt like a prisoner of my circumstances at times. A seemingly normal life can be turned upside down in a day, and you're forced to helplessly suffer through. During Christian's early months I felt abandoned and alone, thrown into a pit of helplessness and left to die, so to speak. My pain flooded me, and I couldn't tread water long enough to gulp in the air of God's goodness before sinking again.

Joseph waited fourteen years before he saw God turn his pain into something good.

After five years I'm still discovering how God turns pain into something beautiful, but I already see how God is redeeming our story. He took the pain and throttled us forward into amazing opportunities that never would have—or could have—happened without that pain. He moved us from the NICU horrors to television airways. My sweet little boy, whom some simultaneously pity and loathe, is now the "Super-Christian" hero of a book and a social media star in his own right.

In Joseph's case he used the power of his position to bless his brothers, bestowing on them food, supplies, and gifts. In the same way I pray that I always help and encourage others.

God has shown us His love and grace in many ways—not necessarily by redeeming or restoring Christian's sight, but by allowing me to comprehend how special it is that He chose me to be Christian's mom. I have the privilege and honor to hold that little boy every single day. My heart still hurts from time to time, but most days are simply full of joy and laughter. Sometimes God restores by giving us the gift of refreshment, of appreciating each new day and the blessings it brings.

We serve a God who cares about our everyday moments, but our ultimate redemption came through

Christ when He died on the cross and rose from the grave, crushing the enemy under His heel. Because Jesus made the ultimate sacrifice, we can experience salvation and spend eternity in heaven.

You can be confident, as the apostle Paul wrote, that He who began a good work in you will carry it on to completion until the day of Christ Jesus (Phil. 1:6). Your journey may look different from mine, but no matter how long the road to redemption is, whether we see the fulfillment of God's promise in our lifetime or not, we can trust that He is performing a good work.

The promise in Scripture is that God remembers our pain.

He restores the years.

He redeems.

SEE GOD...

What areas of your life have you seen God redeem? Ask God to search your heart and show you the areas where you may be holding on to hurt. Allow Him access to redeem that pain and turn it into something good.

_____

_____

Give It to God in Prayer

Father, You are the ultimate Redeemer, the Giver of all good things. Even when I walk through difficult seasons, help me to remember that the things that were intended to harm me, You can redeem for my good. I submit fully to Your will. In Jesus's name, amen.

CONCLUSION

EMBEDDED IN THE word *hope* is the sense of expectation. After journeying through these forty days, my prayer is that you've seen your level of expectation rise and that you have a new awareness of what God can and will do for you when troubles come.

I pray you have gained new confidence that God is in complete control and He is not blindsided by the adversity that comes our way.

He will give you strength for the journey and encourage your heart.

He will guide you through every storm.

He will see you through.

The blessing that Chris and I have clung to is that God is good and He is with us. Sometimes that's all we know for sure, but it's enough. A good God will guide us to the light at the end of the tunnel. An amazing God will give us comfort and peace along the way.

Our heavenly Father is more than great and amazing. He is the omniscient, sovereign almighty God who takes away the sin of the world and in its place leaves hope.

NOTES

INTRODUCTION

1. Craig D. Lounsbrough, *An Intimate Collision: Encounters with Life and Jesus*, as quoted at GoodReads.com, "An Intimate Collision Quotes," accessed December 28, 2016, https://www.goodreads.com/work/quotes/43561163-an-intimate-collision-encounters-with-life-and-jesus?page=2.

DAY 1: RISE ON EAGLES' WINGS

2. Learner.org, "Bald Eagle: How Eagles Fly," accessed December 28, 2016, https://www.learner.org/jnorth/tm/eagle/EagleFlightLesson.html; see also YouTube.com, "How Does an Eagle Fly? Deadly 60, Series 2, BBC, accessed December 28, 2016, https://www.youtube.com/watch?v=tM2bC6qNksM. Berean Publishers, "7 Principles of an Eagle," accessed December 28, 2016, http://www.bereanpublishers.com/7-principles-of-an-eagle/.

Day 9: Look Beyond Your Circumstances

1. C. S. Lewis, *A Grief Observed* (New York: Harper One, 1994), 43.

Day 13: You Are Awesome

1. Lori Stanley Roeleveld, *Running from a Crazy Man (and Other Adventures Traveling with Jesus)* (Raleigh, NC: Lighthouse Publishing of the Carolinas, 2014), 13.

Day 19: Train-Wreck Moments

1. Lisa Bevere, Facebook post, August 20, 2016, accessed November 22, 2016, https://www.facebook.com/lisabevere.page/posts/10157209201965447.

Day 24: The Blessing of Friendship

1. Charles Stanley, "Jesus: Our Best Friend," InTouch.org, January 7, 2016, accessed November 29, 2016, https://www.intouch.org/read/magazine/daily-devotions/jesus-our-best-friend.

Day 30: You Are His Masterpiece

1. Louvre, "The Louvre Welcomes 8.6 Million Visitors in 2015," January 28, 2016, accessed November 30,

2016, http://presse.louvre.fr/86-millions-de-visiteurs-aumusee-du-louvre-en-2015_5037_5037/.

2. Lorena Muñoz-Alonso, "Leonardo da Vinci's 'Mona Lisa' Has Another Portrait Hidden Underneath," Artnet News, December 8, 2015, accessed November 30, 2016, https://news.artnet.com/art-world/leonardo-da-vinci-mona-lisa-portrait-hidden-388235.

Day 31: The Power of Community

1. Rick Warren, *The Purpose-Driven Life* (Grand Rapids, MI: Zondervan, 2002), 141.

Day 32: Willing to Learn

1. Special Kids Therapy and Nursing Center, "Changing Lives Through Jesus Christ," accessed December 30, 2016, http://www.specialkidstn.com/about-us/#changing-lives.

Day 37: World-Changers

1. YouTube.com, "Social Conformity—Brain Games," accessed December 30, 2016, https://www.youtube.com/watch?v=o8BkzvP19v4&feature=youtu.be.

Day 39: Choosing Forgiveness

1. R. T. Kendall, *Total Forgiveness* (Lake Mary, FL: Charisma House, 2002, 2007), 33.

CONNECT WITH US!

CHARISMA HOUSE

(Spiritual Growth)

- Facebook.com/CharismaHouse
- @CharismaHouse
- Instagram.com/CharismaHouse

(Health)

- Pinterest.com/CharismaHouse

MODERN ENGLISH VERSION

(Bible)
www.mevbible.com

SUBSCRIBE TODAY

Exclusive Content

Inspiring Messages

Encouraging Articles

Discovering Freedom

CHARISMA MEDIA

FREE NEWSLETTERS
to experience the power of the *Holy Spirit*

Charisma Magazine Newsletter
Get top-trending articles, Christian teachings, entertainment reviews, videos, and more.

Charisma News Weekly
Get the latest breaking news from an evangelical perspective every Monday.

SpiritLed Woman
Receive amazing stories, testimonies, and articles on marriage, family, prayer, and more.

New Man
Get articles and teaching about the realities of living in the world today as a man of faith.

3-in-1 Daily Devotionals
Find personal strength and encouragement with these devotionals, and begin your day with God's Word.

Sign up for Free at nl.charismamag.com

www.ingramcontent.com/pod-product-compliance
Lightning Source LLC
Chambersburg PA
CBHW060518100426
42743CB00009B/1366